Praying for the dawn

Dedicated to the Iona Community Prayer Circle

Praying for the dawn

A resource book for the ministry of healing

Ruth Burgess & Kathy Galloway (eds)

WILD GOOSE PUBLICATIONS
www.ionabooks.com

First published 2000, reprinted 2007 by

Wild Goose Publications
4th Floor, Savoy House, 140 Sauchiehall Street, Glasgow G2 3DH, Scotland

Wild Goose Publications is the publishing division of the Iona Community.
Scottish Charity No. SCO03794. Limited Company Reg. No. SCO96243.

ISBN 978-1-901557-26-8

Cover illustration © 2000 David Gregson

Overseas distribution:
Australia: Willow Connection Pty Ltd, Unit 4A, 3–9 Kenneth Rd, Manly Vale, NSW 2093
New Zealand: Pleroma, Higginson Street, Otane 4170, Central Hawkes Bay
Canada: Novalis/Bayard Publishing & Distribution, 10 Lower Spadina Ave., Suite 400, Toronto, Ontario M5V 2Z

Printed by Bell & Bain, Thornliebank, Glasgow

Contents

Praying for the dawn

The ministry of healing in the life and worship of the Church

Resources for worship

Concern (C)

Requests (C)

Offering (C)

Endings (D)

Introduction

Since its beginning, the ministry of healing has played a vital and central part in the life of the Iona Community. The healing of broken bodies, painful memories, divided communities and nations, the healing of the earth itself and of our relationship with it, are all part of the integrity to which God calls us. They are all part of the ministry of healing.

Therefore it is a ministry in which justice is as important as medicine, in which reverence for the earth is as vital as respect for the individual person and in which the health of the body politic matters as much as the health of the body personal. Indeed, they are inextricably linked.

The ministry of healing is not only an exterior one. We are also invited to the healing of the divisions and splits in our own lives; the separation of the spiritual and the material is simply not possible if we believe that Jesus really lived in the flesh, was incarnate, made holy and whole the broken human body. So we cannot separate our actions from their consequences, our freedom from our responsibility, our lives as individuals from our lives as persons in community.

We are invited into the community of God. This community, we believe, extends over the limitations of time and space. We are part of the communion of saints; our wholeness is inclusive, not exclusive. Even in death we are not divided.

We have, at the invitation of the Iona Community's publishing division, Wild Goose Publications, sought in this book to show something of the background, context and range of the healing ministry of the Community. The essays and liturgies reflect involvement in the National Health Service (in which many of our members work), in social and community work, as artists and theologians, in local church ministry with people who are ill, and in a wide range of justice and peace campaigning. We understand all of these as being part of the gospel imperative of healing.

We have also sought to offer quite detailed resources for those who wish to introduce the ministry of healing in a more intentional way but are not sure where to start. We hope that these guidelines, based on many years of experience of planning and leading services of prayer for healing and the laying-on of hands, and of leading Bible studies and discussions on healing, both on Iona and elsewhere, may give some the confidence to go on and discover their own insights and experience in this work.

We also offer a selection of prayers, readings, meditations and blessings which can be used in the ways suggested, or as seems appropriate. We are grateful to all those in the Community and beyond who have allowed us to share these rich resources with others.

Ruth Burgess and Kathy Galloway

Using this book

In most of the liturgies, suggestions are made for scripture readings. These are not set in stone, and alternative readings, perhaps from a lectionary or appropriate to the occasion, may be used. Similarly, in most of the liturgies, songs and hymns are suggested. These are almost all taken from *Common Ground*, the new ecumenical songbook recently produced in Scotland (and in which members of the Community are represented). As an ecumenical community, we want to encourage the discovery of the wealth of one another's singing traditions, and we commend the book. But many of the songs are available in other collections, or other songs may be equally appropriate.

Throughout the book, those parts for a single voice are given in lower case normal type, and those for all to join in are given in capitals. Directions are given in italics.

The Church's healing ministry

The Church's healing ministry

Kate McIlhagga

Healing is something we all long for. Healing is something God longs for.

The God who created the galaxies (and us) must hover over that creation, like a mother over a baby in a pram, and yearn for goodness and wholeness and health and security and happiness for it. The biblical record shows how the God of creation, the God who led people out of political captivity and spoke to them through the prophets, was constantly seeking new ways to achieve wholeness or *salvation* for the created order.

The word *salvation* comes from the same root as that of health and wholeness. However we interpret the biblical doctrine of the Fall – and there are many variations on that theme, ranging from snakes and ladders to the idea of a crack in the mirror – we all sense that, although we as women and men are made in the image of God, we are lacking something; there is imperfection, we are less than whole.

If we are Christians we believe that when the God who created matter became matter, became incarnate in Jesus, Emmanuel, God-with-us, something happened; something which rocked the creation to its core and affected each individual in the most intimate way.

Again the images are endless. Christ is seen as the bridge-builder, the suffering servant, the liberator, the healer; we all have our favourites. When we talk therefore of the Church's God-given ministry of healing, we are not talking about something for the cranky way-out few, but about an aspect of salvation history which is essential to the wellbeing of the nations and of Mrs Smith in the run-down cottage across the road.

The healing ministry is first and foremost about justice and peace – about the healing of the nations. But intertwined with that divine imperative is the healing of the individual, the healing of memory, of broken relationships. Always within the context of the community of the church or the family or the society the healing of broken minds and bodies is seen as a God-given task for Christ's disciples in every age.

Some would say it has been a neglected ministry. I would suggest it has always been present where the church has offered sanctuary, forgiveness and, above all, the Eucharist in any community, but it is a ministry which needs highlighting and focusing. In our age, as in any other, the healing ministry of Christ's body, the church, has to engage with and grapple with the problem of suffering and pain, which is the experience of so many people in the world. We cannot trivialise it by saying, 'Never mind, your pain will make you a better person,' or bypass it by saying, 'You may not understand, but in God's greater plan your suffering is acceptable.' Nor can we zap it with magic. The church is not into mumbo-jumbo. We have to take it seriously and it is only when we take the mystery of suffering seriously that we begin to see the face of Christ in it all. Healing is not about curing – it is about wholeness. Health is not about perfection but about reconciliation.

Service of prayers for healing, including the laying-on of hands

(This order has been used regularly in Iona Abbey for the weekly service of prayers for healing and the laying-on of hands)

Introduction

Opening responses

We come in this service to God
IN OUR NEED, AND BRINGING WITH US THE NEEDS OF THE WORLD
We come to God, who comes to us in Jesus
AND WHO KNOWS BY EXPERIENCE WHAT HUMAN LIFE IS LIKE
We come with our faith and with our doubts
WE COME WITH OUR HOPES AND WITH OUR FEARS
We come as we are, because it is God who invites us to come
AND GOD HAS PROMISED NEVER TO TURN US AWAY

Song

Reading

Prayers of approach and intercession

Song
During the singing of this song, those who wish to receive the laying-on of hands are asked to come and take a place at one of the kneelers set out, and those who wish to share in this ministry should also come out and stand behind those who kneel. If all the places are occupied, please wait with those standing, and after the first group have received the laying-on of hands, they will move back to allow others to take their place. Those standing are invited to place a hand on the shoulder of those standing or kneeling in front of them, as a way of physically sharing in the prayers.

Prayer for the laying-on of hands

SPIRIT OF THE LIVING GOD, PRESENT WITH US NOW
ENTER YOU, BODY, MIND AND SPIRIT,
AND HEAL YOU OF ALL THAT HARMS YOU
IN JESUS' NAME. AMEN

Benediction

Watch now, dear Lord, with those who wake or watch or weep tonight, and give your angels charge over those who sleep. Tend your sick ones, O Lord Christ, rest your weary ones, bless your dying ones, soothe your suffering ones, pity your afflicted ones, shield your joyous ones, and all for your love's sake. AMEN
(St Augustine)

And now may the God of hope fill us with all joy and peace in believing, that we may abound in hope in the power of the Holy Spirit. AMEN

The service of prayers for healing of the Iona Community
A historical and theological perspective
W. Graham Monteith

A healing service has been part of the Iona Community's witness for over sixty years. This is no mean achievement considering the instability of healing services in general. Why has the healing service on Iona and the Community's commitment to the Prayer Circle lasted so long? The answer lies in the fact that it is grounded in the life of the world and is not dependent on spectacular miracles to prove that God's presence and action pervades this service. It is now a major task to maintain the Iona Prayer Circle and the role of Prayer Circle secretary is a permanent appointment within the Community.

The service has never been dependent on one person's leadership and throughout most of the years it has been open to be shared by many.

The custom of holding regular intercessory services for named individuals or causes appears to have evolved rather than being a deliberate policy. No doubt it was spurred on by the outbreak of war in 1939. The theological perspective of the Founder of the Community, the Very Reverend Lord MacLeod of Fuinary, led him to adopt the need for healing by intercession and the laying-on of hands. Ralph Morton, the theologian who was for many years the Deputy Leader, wrote at an early stage of this commitment within the context of the Iona Community:

> *With the coming of the Community to Iona in 1938 there came requests for prayers for healing. These requests were always met. Prayers were made for the sick and a list put up in the Abbey of those for whom prayers were asked. Why did these requests come to Iona? They are often from people quite unknown. The memory of Iona as a place of healing was not dead. Men of old had come to Iona because it was a centre of Christian life. And it was when again there was an active life in the Abbey that requests for prayer came in again. It was not the place but the life that made prayer possible.*[1]

George MacLeod often referred to Iona as the 'Lourdes of Scotland'. Just as the Abbey was being rebuilt in an act of faith, so were broken bodies committed to God's healing power in order that they might be rebuilt and made whole.

From the beginning the Prayer List on Iona was designed to attract names from all over the world.[2] Those from the UK were expected to report progress or needs weekly, whilst people from overseas were required to write every third week. The current organisation of the intercessions for the Iona Prayer Circle and the healing service work in two ways. Prayer requests can be made in person, by letter or by telephone, until 5 pm on the night of the service. This list is used during the service and then left in St Columba's Chapel until the following service. The Prayer List that is drawn up for the Prayer Circle is circulated throughout the UK and is used after the main service and by intercessors who receive it at regular intervals.

The most outstanding feature of the healing service is its inclusiveness, both in its order which seeks to involve everyone, and in the open-endedness of the situations for which prayer may be offered. Ron Ferguson, a former Leader of the Community, writes making a connection with the form of confession which has always been characteristic of the Community's worship:

> *The laying on of hands is not exercised by one person, but by the whole community – and the leader of worship kneels to receive the hands of the community (just as in the Community's morning office the leader of worship confesses his or her sins and hears the absolution pronounced by the whole congregation).*[3]

There is good reason to quote here part of a sermon by Archbishop, now Cardinal, Thomas Winning. His words were recorded by Ron Ferguson at the healing service during the week of the Ecumenical Conference in 1984 which drew together all the church leaders in Scotland. He appropriately chose to make this statement during the healing service and grasped the prevailing openness of the service even to the healing of denominational divisions.

> *The path to further reconciliation to my mind cannot lie in brooding over our wounds, or in mutual recriminations, but in a continual series of creative experiments born of goodwill and with a vision of the future which we are building together. The churches have therefore above all to be open to the unifying power of the Spirit. If we are static, immobile, motionless, there will be no room for the Spirit. If the Church is static, it will not command the response from the Lord to come to its aid. But against a Church on the move, open to the Spirit, the gates of hell will never prevail.*[4]

The service has always given participants the opportunity to place before God people with illnesses, situations with discord, and nations broken by strife.

The opening responses of the regular healing service underscore the theme of solidarity of the people with God, and with his world:

Leader   We come in this service to God,
ALL   IN OUR NEED, AND BRINGING WITH US THE NEEDS OF THE WORLD.
Leader   We come to God, who has come to us in Jesus,
ALL   AND WHO KNOWS BY EXPERIENCE WHAT HUMAN LIFE IS LIKE.
Leader   We come with our faith and with our doubts.
ALL   WE COME WITH OUR HOPES AND WITH OUR FEARS.
Leader   We come as we are, because it is God who invites us to come,
ALL   AND GOD HAS PROMISED NEVER TO TURN US AWAY.[5]

This part of the liturgy emphasises some key elements of the Iona Community's present theology of healing:

- Healing and wholeness concern not only the individual but the world.
- God through Jesus Christ is with us, and the world, in all our experience of life.
- Healing is sought through our own volition but granted by the will of God.
- An unquestioning faith is not a precondition of healing.
- God is always in solidarity with us.

The theology of Jean Vanier, a Canadian theologian and founder in France of l'Arche Community, is evident in the World Council of Churches' thinking on health and wholeness, and there are obvious parallels in the liturgy and hymns of the Iona Community. In the morning office the entire congregation in the Abbey on Iona is asked to 'confess to God and in the company of all God's people that my life and the life of the world are broken by my sin.' Vanier grounds brokenness in the Fall but identifies human suffering in the rejection by society of so many who are socially disadvantaged or unacceptable.

Our God is a God of life and light.
When God creates, it is life and light that is given.
To understand the depth of our brokenness
we need to look at the wholeness in which we were created,
a wholeness that comes from total communion with God. [6]

It is the deep embrace of all who suffer, who are battered or buffeted by society, which gives Vanier's writings their appeal.

The liturgy of healing in the Iona Community is more than just the compilation, the recitation, of a service. It is a vehicle for the expression of many talents. Members have written numerous hymns which have spoken strongly of human brokenness. The most obvious of many might be *A Touching Place* by John L. Bell and Graham Maule. Members have brought their experience of caring to the service, whilst countless prayer secretaries have devotedly arranged prayer lists.

The Iona Community also has many members who are engaged in the healing professions. MacMillan nurses, health visitors and doctors have not abandoned the healing service but have embraced it. They have brought from their practices insights into healing and wholeness. They have identified the limits of medicine and the experience of healing in those who have found peace beyond the comfort of medicine.

Others have worked in communities fraught with conflict and tension, be it Palestine or racially explosive areas of our inner cities. Many members have visited Northern Ireland, and the Corrymeela Community there, and have brought back the conviction that prayer and common life offers reconciliation and peace. International concerns are reflected in the use of songs like Fred Kaan's *For the Healing of the Nations*.

We witness the pastoral concern of George MacLeod; or the creative and innovative thinking of John Bell or the focusing of latent concerns drawn from personal experience by Anna Briggs. The language is always changing and assimilating new ideas and influences. For example, Margaret Stewart, a doctor and minister, summed up the assimilation of several such concepts in her introduction to a healing service in 1996:

For me to understand the significance of healing I do not look at the drama of miraculous stories, biblical or contemporary. For me all healing is amazing, miraculous if you like. The process by which our bodies and minds can be repaired fills me with awe. The complexity of the process of repair of even a small cut, a minor upset seems to me so much more wonderful because it happens from within. The potential for wholeness and fullness of life is present within individual cells of our bodies.

[She goes on to write of the laying-on of hands] …*we come forward with concern for our lack of wholeness, for family and friends, for broken community and by our action in asking and accepting the hands of the people who travel alongside us tonight we open ourselves to the power of the healing spirit. Such can energise the healing process present in our bodies* [my emphasis], *our minds and our spirits.*

Often often often comes Christ in the stranger's guise.[7] [line quoted from a Celtic Rune]

Peter Millar, a former Warden of the Abbey, believes that this age is characterised by plurality which allows many different belief systems to coexist in a pick-and-mix fashion. Religion today offers many different kinds of authority and can leave people totally confused or searching for understanding. Even visitors who trek across Mull to Iona often have no clear conception of what Iona may be about.

He argues that people in a post-modern age are more inclined to seek a 'direct' experience of God and may invest their search in a quest for healing. It is almost more natural to seek this personal experience now than it was in the days of George MacLeod because religious practice is not dependent upon the specific authority of a minister or any other agent. It is not all-encompassing but may be just one part of a person's religious life. He writes of direct experience:

I also believe that we are discovering (or rather rediscovering) the power of prayer in healing. This is partly because the modern mind, in my opinion, wants a direct experience of the divine rather than some mediated experience. Within post modernism there is this search for the transcendent; we cannot live in a world denuded of transcendence. I think also that healing is seen to be important in many lives because of a greater recognition of evil/darkness/threatening powers. Many people want to be 'healed' and what they mean is taken out of their 'inner darkness' which they feel powerfully.[8]

The service of healing born on Iona out of a crisis, that of the Second World War, has sustained itself for fifty years, which is no small achievement when most healing revivals tend to be short-lived, dependent upon the charisma of one central figure and fed by evidence of healing which is apparent to all. The liturgy deliberately makes no reference to a leader, nor does it offer any evidential results. The healing service has its critics, yet no one has been sufficiently disillusioned to topple the overriding confidence in its propriety and logicality within the context of a concern for ensuring *'in all things the purpose of our community, that hidden things may be revealed to us and new ways found to touch the hearts of all.'*[9] There is a conviction, and a manifest emotional feeling, that the service touches the hearts of participants and still commands a central place in the overall strategy of the Community.

References

1   Morton, T.R., *Divine Healing*, in *The Coracle*, July 1952, No 22, p21
2   MacLeod, G.F., *Practical Suggestions for Intercessions for the Sick*, GM & ICP, National Library of Scotland, Acc9084/337[M]
3   Ferguson, R., *Chasing the Wild Goose*, Fount, Glasgow 1988, p192
4   ibid
5   The Iona Community, *The Iona Community Worship Book*, Wild Goose Publications Glasgow 1988, p37
6   Vanier, J. *The Broken Body*, DLT, London 1988, p1
7   Abstracted from Margaret Stewart's notes in preparation for the healing service of 30/7/1996
8   Millar, P.W., correspondence dated 7/8/1996
9   Iona Community, *Prayer for the Iona Community*, in *Members' Handbook*, published yearly by the Iona Community

Pilgrim liturgy for healing

(Written for a pilgrimage to Whitby Abbey, but may be adapted for other places)

Reader

Pilgrimage is traditionally a journey to a holy place – a place where saints have walked, a place where God has met people and blessed them.

People through the ages have journeyed with God on pilgrimage – to perform a penance, to ask for healing, to pray for places where there is war or national disaster, to pray for friends.

Pilgrimage is an opportunity to travel lightly, to walk free of daily routines, to meet people, to make friends, to enjoy and celebrate God's creation. An opportunity too in the travelling, the conversations and the silences to reflect on the journey of our lives and on our journey homewards to God.

Prayers before setting out on pilgrimage

God of the guiding star, the bush that blazes
SHOW US YOUR WAY
God of the stormy seas, the bread that nourishes
TEACH US YOUR TRUTH
God of the still, small voice, the wind that blows where it chooses
FILL US WITH LIFE
God of the elements, of our inward and outward journeys
SET OUR FEET ON YOUR ROAD TODAY

MAY GOD BLESS US WITH A SAFE JOURNEY
MAY THE ANGELS AND SAINTS TRAVEL WITH US
MAY WE LIVE THIS DAY IN JUSTICE AND JOY
AMEN

Prayers at Whitby

I was glad when they said to me
LET US GO INTO GOD'S HOUSE
Friends and strangers, travellers and pilgrims
LET US GO INTO GOD'S HOUSE
For in this place, as in all creation
GOD WELCOMES US WITH LOVE

Song *Sing for God's glory   (Common Ground)*

Prayers of approach

We are here God, here where you have brought us.
In our laughter and struggling,
you have travelled with us;
in rocks and flowers
we have glimpsed you and known you,
Loving God our Maker
WE ARE GLAD TO BE HERE WITH YOU

We are here Jesus, here where you have called us.
In our questioning and listening,
you have travelled with us;
in stories and shared bread
we have recognised you and loved you,
Jesus Christ our friend and brother.
WE ARE GLAD TO BE HERE WITH YOU

We are here, Holy Spirit, here where you have led us.
In our doubting and our longing,
you have travelled with us;
in the love of friends and strangers
we have known you and blessed you,
Holy Spirit our comforter and disturber
WE ARE GLAD TO BE HERE WITH YOU

We are here God, and there are others here with us;
angels who have walked with us,
saints who have been here before us,

little ones who have met us on our way.
Gathered with your people,
warmed with the wonder of your welcome
WE ARE GLAD TO BE HERE WITH YOU

You know us, God.
You made us, you love us.
You know the worst and the best about us.
You know what hurts us.
You know how we hurt others.
You know what keeps us away from you.
In the silence of this moment,
we ask you to meet us and heal us,
to bring us close to you.
(Silence)
God have mercy on us
CHRIST HAVE MERCY ON US

Listen to the words of Jesus, words that we can trust:
'Don't be afraid.
I love you, I forgive you,
you are my friends, I will always be with you.
Come and follow me.'

Thanks be to God
AMEN

Psalm 122
We were glad when they said to us:
'Let us go to the house of the Lord.'

And now our feet are standing:
within your gates, O Jerusalem;

Jerusalem which is built as a city:
where the pilgrims gather in unity.

There the tribes go up, the tribes of the Lord:
as he commanded Israel, to give thanks to the name of the Lord.

There are set thrones of judgement:
the thrones of the house of David.

O pray for the peace of Jerusalem:
may those who love you prosper.

Peace be within your walls:
and prosperity in your palaces.

For the sake of our kindred and companions:
we will pray that peace be with you.

For the sake of the house of the Lord our God:
we will seek for your good.

(Taken from the Liturgical Psalter – New Inclusive Language Version)

New Testament reading
Colossians 1:9b–12

Story of Hilda

Story of Caedmon

Synod of Whitby
(Taken from Bede, A history of the English Church and people)

Prayers for ourselves and others
(This may be accompanied by the lighting of candles)
ending with…

Christ is the morning star
who, when the night of this world is past
brings to his saints
the promise of the light of life
and opens everlasting day.
(Bede)

Song *One more step (Common Ground)*

Hilda's blessing

Have peace with one another
as children of one mother
let each defer to other
and may your hearts be one

Have peace with all around you
sweet love of earth surround you
and may no harm confound you
or break the peace within

Have peace with God your maker
in Jesus be partaker
and Spirit consecrator
God, three in one, grant peace

The peace of God possess you
the love of God caress you
the grace of heaven bless you
peace everlastingly

Prayers at the end of a pilgrimage

For the joy of God's creation, for the friendship of God's people
WE GIVE THANKS
For a day of prayers and stories, for a journey safely ended
WE GIVE THANKS
For the love of God within us, for the hope that shines before us
WE GIVE THANKS

And now, and for all our days, in the words of St Hilda, we ask God's
blessing on our lives as we say together
MAY THE PEACE OF GOD POSSESS US
THE LOVE OF GOD CARESS US
THE GRACE OF HEAVEN BLESS US
PEACE EVERLASTINGLY
AMEN

Additional alternative prayers and collects of the saints

The water of baptism is the fresh growth of the world
 and is called the fount of the healing oil of faith.
*(T.M. Charles Edwards, lines from a poem about St Winifred's Well,
Holywell – Tudor Aled, 1840–1926)*

O most merciful Redeemer, Friend, Brother
may we know thee more clearly,
love thee more dearly,
follow thee more nearly
for ever and ever. Amen
(St Richard of Chichester, died 1253)

Alone with none but thee, my God
I journey on my way.
What need I fear when thou art near,
O King of night and day?
More safe am I within thy hand
than if a host did round me stand.
(Attributed to St Columba)

The love of your creator be with you.
Great God, grant us your light
Great God, grant us your grace
Great God, grant us your joy
and let us be made pure in the well of your health.
(Carmina Gaedelica)

Healing the wounds of the body politic

The National Health Service and the health of the nation

Allan Gordon

In 1998, the National Health Service (NHS) celebrated its fiftieth birthday. This means that the majority of the British population have no experience of what healthcare was like before the formation of the NHS. Then, calling out a doctor meant having to pay directly out of one's own pocket for healthcare. For the poor or less well-off, there was often great reluctance to call out or attend the doctor because of the cost, and so at times medical help was sought too late.

Background

One of the great founding principles of the new NHS, stated by the then Minister of Health, Aneurin Bevan, was that 'the quality of your healthcare should not depend upon your ability to pay for it'. The intention of the new NHS was to eliminate such inequalities. So today an unwaged person who requires major cancer surgery and expensive chemotherapy will get the same quality of treatment as their wealthy counterpart with a similar illness. It is both privilege and imperative to be able to treat people on the basis of their need without any regard to their ability to pay for it, and to provide the best treatment for all. The NHS is the envy of many other countries. It is worth saving and fighting for. However, it is often only when we become patients ourselves that we really appreciate the qualities of our health service. Even if only because we or those we love may need its care one day, it is important that we do all we can to safeguard it now.

The NHS is now the second largest employer in the world. Although Britain spends far less per head on healthcare than many other developed countries, nevertheless the cost is enormous and the NHS has to operate within financial constraints set by the government of the day. The very successes of the NHS in providing healthcare, and the fact that new, better treatments are always being developed and that people are living longer has meant that demands for healthcare are increasing year on year. The health service has never had sufficient resources to meet all the expectations or demands placed on it. And so, increasingly, difficult questions needed to be answered about the priorities for the use of limited resources. Politicians from different parties may have very diverse views on how these resources should be targeted.

Politicians and priorities

The constraints on public spending in the last years of the Conservative government of the early 1990s led in real terms to lower than inflation increases in health spending. There was a real pressure to get value for money and eliminate inefficient practices. New administrators were brought in to achieve this. Sadly, most of the extra year by year finance provided by central government had to go to support staff pay rises, and often these were not fully funded so that the extra had to be made up locally, resulting in even more financial pressures. Little additional money was available to cope with greater workload. This led to the closure of smaller hospitals and individual wards, so other parts of the service could be funded. It soon became apparent that the new administrators found it difficult to manage doctors who were used to exerting their clinical freedom, and the seemingly endless needs of patients. Increasingly senior doctors were drawn into management roles themselves. But whoever is in this role has to cope constantly with the major problem of underfunding.

The Labour government of the late 1990s set different priorities for the NHS – such as reducing waiting lists and improving the quality of care. On the surface these seem like admirable goals. However, the numbers of patients being seen each year continues to increase (in some areas by up to 8 per cent on the previous year). Without extra facilities, doctors, nurses and support staff it is difficult to cope with these increasing numbers and yet at the same time reduce waiting lists. The government did provide extra waiting list initiative money but decisions about its use were not necessarily based on clinical need. Rather than treating the few with more disabling major problems, some of the money was spent on the many patients with minor disorders because by doing so waiting list numbers were seen to be dropping.

The government plans for improving the quality of care have been spelt out in a paper entitled 'A First Class Service'. The public have a right to expect that the quality of care they receive from the NHS is of a high standard. New initiatives are being introduced to monitor the clinical competence of doctors. No one, for example, would expect a civil aviation pilot, fully trained at age 30, to continue to fly the public in airliners until retirement age without regular retraining and reassessment courses. Similarly, many of the medical Royal Colleges have introduced compulsory medical education, be it a minimum of fifty hours a year attending medical conferences or some form of continuous professional development. These changes have been welcomed and are being further developed by the General Medical Council in a scheme known as revalidation.

A changing health service

The health service continues to change. Newer, better but more costly drugs to treat various ailments are always becoming available. Newer surgical techniques requiring costly equipment and expensive investigative procedures are constantly being developed. Disorders that had few options for cure many years ago can now be dealt with more effectively. These new treatments are not cheap, but are very effective alternatives. There is also the demand to replace ageing, obsolete and worn-out medical equipment, and this again can be very costly, especially with regard to items found in X-ray departments or in intensive care units, where it is common for new equipment to cost in excess of £500,000.

A danger of too tight an economic squeeze on NHS finances is that a degree of 'rationing', or, to use the more politically correct term, 'priority setting' will grow. An example of this occurs in the area of infertility. Some infertile couples can only achieve a pregnancy by using the technique of in-vitro fertilisation (IVF). This is expensive, however, and so some Health Boards refuse to provide it on the NHS, while others do. So whether a couple qualify for IVF funded by the NHS could depend on their postal code! This has led to inequalities in care, because although some couples can afford to self-fund their IVF through private treatment, this is not an option available to the less well-off. These changes are very much against the ideal of the NHS. The quality of care should not depend on the individual's ability to pay for it.

Staff

The staff of the NHS – doctors, nurses, midwives, auxiliaries, porters, receptionists, physiotherapists and all the others who ensure this great social provision – are overwhelmingly marked by their professionalism and dedication. Doctors have traditionally worked long hours, and junior doctors especially may work all day, be up all night caring for emergency admissions and then work all the following day. There is great job satisfaction in providing clinical care; however, the expansion in workload without a concomitant boost in resources has led to a great increase in the strain and pressures on all staff. Nurses in particular may feel it is difficult to provide the same level of good care to expanding numbers of patients. In hospital, the faster movement of patients from Acute Receiving Units to other wards and thence home can make it more difficult for nurses to build good relationships with them. It is essential that considerate attention is given to the needs of our nurses and midwives because both in hospital and in the community they are such a vital component of the health service.

An increasing pressure on doctors is the medico-legal one – the risk of being sued for medical negligence. A leading lawyer said on the radio recently that 'everyone makes mistakes'. However, no one wants the doctor treating them to make a mistake, and if it happens they may sue. So there is added pressure on medical staff to try to make every consultation, diagnosis and treatment perfect. The Royal Medical Colleges and relevant government departments have been increasingly supportive of the need for the profession to be aware of best practice. A series of 'Effective Clinical Guidelines' detailing good practice for a wide variety of disorders has been published and is regularly updated. As doctors keep up to date with expert opinion on the diagnosis and management of medical conditions, the hope is that good practice may reduce medico-legal risks.

General practice

For the majority of the public, their first point of contact with the health service is through their general practitioner (GP) working in the community (Primary Care Services). GPs have a very broad knowledge of medical disorders and where they wish a further opinion on management they can refer the patient to the appropriate hospital specialist. Good relationships between GPs and specialists are an important link between care in the community and in the hospital, especially where much GP time is taken up with an increasingly elderly population and in the management of chronic illnesses.

Sucessive governments have also introduced much change to general practice, and for many GPs there has already been too much change, introduced too quickly and without adequate consultation. Few GPs have ever been trained in management or budget control and yet responsibility for budgets has been devolved to them, with pressure to use limited sums more efficiently. Here too this may mean looking at where to save money to fund staff pay rises. Prescribing has also been subject to change, with similar pressure on finance and doctors being told what they may and may not prescribe. The same factors that have led to the amalgamation or closure of smaller hospitals have also seen many smaller GP practices amalgamating. Doctors may be on call less, reducing often lengthy hours of work, yet for the public it means that patients who need a GP for an emergency are less likely to see their own GP overnight or at weekends. The longstanding desire that Primary Care Services should have more time to promote and improve the health of their own local populations remains as strong as ever.

Support

Working in the health service can be immensely satisfying. The British people do generally get a very high standard of care from a committed and professional staff who work under enormous pressure, and who, at times, feel that they do not get the support that they deserve from the politicians and media. Bad news makes better copy than good news, and the health service is no exception in this. The many disorders that are cured or made significantly better get no headlines. And the newer and better methods for diagnosis and treatment worth celebrating may, because of under-resourcing, be being introduced more slowly than they ought to be. Nevertheless, it is certainly worth fighting for an NHS that treats patients on the basis of their need and to a high standard. In particular, there is a real challenge to promote those things that might lead to a healthier life – for example, good diet, regular exercise, stopping smoking, sensible drinking, and reducing stress levels and dependence on drugs. This would be the best way to combat those cynics who argue that the NHS is the National Illness Service because almost all its budget is spent dealing with illness rather than health.

The future

The future will see initiatives aimed at trying to improve the health of our children and young people. It would be good to see inroads being made into the problems posed by unwanted teenage pregnancies and sexually transmitted diseases. Clearly this may mean introducing new methods of promoting sexual education and more responsible sexual behaviour. Similar initiatives will be necessary to combat the rising dependence on drugs.

Major projects in the new millennium will be aimed at the prevention and early detection and better treatment of major killing diseases like cancer and heart attacks. Local Health Boards are being encouraged to set up Health Improvement programmes so that the local health needs can be identified and addressed.

The challenges posed by ill health remain daunting but are among the most worthwhile to try to meet. Today's health service is underfunded and under-resourced. But it is one of our most precious national assets. The support of all of us for it is essential – even if it is only at the ballot box!

(This article is largely drawn from a talk given to the Iona Community in plenary on Iona, and dedicated to the memory of a previous leader, Rev. Ian Reid. Ian was very supportive of and challenging to a new young medical graduate seeking to integrate Christian beliefs with a medical vocation. The journey has been very interesting and exciting and worthwhile.)

Weeping for cities and working for justice

Ruth Burgess

The Spirit of the Lord is upon me
because he has chosen me to bring good news to the poor.
He has sent me to proclaim liberty to the captives
and recovery of sight to the blind;
To free the oppressed
and announce that the time has come
when the Lord will save his people
(Luke 4:18–21)

When we talk about the healing ministry of the church, often the focus of our discussion is on the healing of individuals who are sick or in need. Issues of hungry people in India or oppressed people in South America, or of people struggling with multiple deprivation in our inner-city communities and housing schemes, are assumed to be the kind of issues that belong in a discussion about peace and justice. They are not normally seen as part of the church's ministry of healing.

I have always asked questions about prayers for healing, and much of my questioning arises from the experience of living and working for many years in British inner cities. To pray for individuals with specific illnesses and needs seemed only to touch the edge of the situation. People's lives are lived in the context of their environment, and to probe the roots of their pain and anger is a process that inevitably leads to the need for change – change that will involve both healing and justice if it is to be any kind of good news for those who live in the inner cities.

The pain of a city is complex. The suffering that cripples our inner cities is often the pain of lifetimes and generations. The pain of individuals is bound up with the pain of the whole community. A battered child is all too often the child of parents who were, in their turn, battered by their parents. When a child is killed on a busy road that runs through a housing estate, or an old person dies of hypothermia because they cannot afford to heat an all-electric flat, the whole community suffers. The community suffers because all their children and all their pensioners are at risk, and will continue to be at risk until there is change.

And how do I pray for healing for this community? When I begin to pray for the individuals I meet, I find myself praying and acting for the whole community. I cannot pray for an old person with bronchitis if I do not also put pressure on a council or a landlord who is responsible for the damp and substandard housing that is the root cause of the illness.

How can I pray for those who are lonely, old and disabled if I do not take time to visit them, and, at the same time, ask why there is so little funding to provide sheltered accommodation and to staff daycentres? I cannot pray for families living in tower-blocks, whose relationships are at breaking-point, and whose children are distressed, if I do not raise questions about the way that government and local authorities allocate housing stock and fund playspace and nursery provision.

I cannot pray for a young person in prison if I do not look for ways to relieve the boredom of unemployment, the pressure of advertising, the board and lodgings legislation that keeps him on the move, and the lure of drugs, that have combined to destroy his liberty. I cannot pray for people who are poor in my community, or for that matter for people who are hungry, oppressed and poor anywhere else in the world, if I do not challenge the way that my country's government spends its resources.

I say I cannot pray. What I mean is that I cannot pray for the healing of others with integrity without also acting on my prayers. If I am blind to the sources of injustice around me, and divorce the needs of an individual from the pain of a whole community, my prayers for healing are non-sense and bear no resemblance to the good news of the gospel.

Has prayer any validity in the context of the cities' pain? Is it not rather naive to spend time in prayer when what is needed is action? What good can prayer do? Most of the people I pray for have no idea that I am praying for them, so what is the point?

I find it much easier to ask these questions than to answer them. When I prayed in the midst of the city, I discovered that my prayer changed me. When I prayed, I let God's love into my life, and the healing and forgiveness that that love brought made it far more possible for me to live out the gospel than if I had not prayed. Prayer made me open to change. It was not a substitute for action; rather the source of action's motivation. Prayer made me aware of God's love for me and for the people around me, and that brought a sense of healing amidst the anger and pain.

But the pain within me and the pain around me did not go away, and the injustice continued and at times overwhelmed me and the community, filling us with rage and frustration and fear.

Jesus, you wept for the city you loved – in your words and actions the oppressed found justice and the angry found release… (prayer heading used on Iona)

Weeping for cities and working for justice is rarely dramatic or sensational. It is not an activity that brings instantaneous results. The suffering of a dispossessed community, in Britain or anywhere else in the world, has no easy solutions. For healing and justice to occur there needs to be change – change in values and attitudes; change in political policies and social conditions. And change for those in need means change for everyone, and none of us change easily.

When we pray for the healing of those around us, are we willing to live out the implications of our prayers?

Jesus, teach us how to pray.

Justice as healing

Kathy Galloway

In 1954, George MacLeod wrote: *Our congregations miss the zest of the early Christian church because we have forgotten the glorious emancipation of our true humanity that was the Incarnation. Jesus the carpenter, the friend of shepherds and fishermen, showed us God by being human – and in three days set at naught the complex temple that was forty years in building. He made risen humanity his temple. We must be human.*

In a new millennium, we are facing a *kairos,* a time of crisis, a defining moment in human history. In the midst of a hugely accelerated pace of change, we are confronting in equal measure unparalleled opportunities and unparalleled threats. Many people, particularly in the West, are healthier, wealthier and enjoy greater opportunities for self-realisation than ever before. At the same time, the gap between rich and poor is growing, significant parts of the human population live on the margins of destitution, uprooted peoples number tens of millions and wars and pandemics devastate dozens of countries. Social and political institutions everywhere are under question, in transition, and once-powerful ideologies have lost their hold. The fabric and future of life itself is under threat: genetic modification and engineering beg many questions, while the wealth of consumer nations and the poverty and exploitation of energy- and resource-poor countries have created an ecological holocaust which threatens the continued existence of the planet.

It is the good news about being human which Jesus brought that is so crucial for the world as we stand on the threshold of a new millennium. We know that religion has always had the power both to heal and to hurt, and our divisions have often been the cause of much of the hurt. But now it is time to put away our ancient prejudices, leave our divisions behind us and draw on our power to heal.

In this *kairos,* this crisis, there is a great temptation to retreat, to hide away in our churches and in a private kind of religion or personal spirituality – a security blanket against all the challenges and difficulties facing us. But in this way, religion continues to be part of the problem. Jesus came to show how much God loved the *world*. So we must turn again *to* the world, and celebrate once more Jesus' good news about being human.

We live in a world which sets value by market forces and whose spirituality is one of value addition, of extrinsic worth. So it is good news to say yes to and to practise Jesus' gospel of *intrinsic worth*, in which all living things, including the earth itself, have innate value separate from and beyond their utility; in which the commodification, the selling, of all of life is resisted and reversed and in which justice is done. To be human in Jesus' way is *to act justly*.

We live in a world of seemingly hostile global forces, of the sense of powerlessness to effect positive change which results in ethnic conflict and resource wars and of the collapse of traditional support structures. So it is good news to say yes to and to practise not de-personalised but *re-person-alised human relationships*, an inclusive respect for the 'other' (neighbour *and* enemy) and new structures of care for the weakest in which the potential of all people, not just 'our people', can be protected. To be human in Jesus' way is *to love kindness*.

We live in a world in which human pride, *hubris,* which thinks of itself as creator rather than created, has come to threaten life on earth. So it is good news to say yes to and to practise a more *self-disciplined ethos of reverence and respect* for cultural, spiritual and bio-diversity alike, in which criteria for the good life are invested less in possession, surfaces and speed and more in appreciation, substance and a sense of the mystery at the heart of life. To be human in Jesus' way is *to walk humbly with God*.

The oil of healing and the salt of friendship

In order for us, as followers of Jesus, to be able to hold out healing, we have our own challenges to face up to. Unless we do, we won't have either the integrity or the credibility to speak with authority, and we will simply imitate the worst prejudices and practices of our society. It would be some-what hypocritical to speak of healing to others if we don't continue to grapple with our own brokenness. We are seeking now, in our time, to heal the hurts of the past, and not just between those of different traditions, but the hurts of people who have found themselves, for whatever reason, shut out by the church. Some of these hurts are still raw and throbbing. They need the soothing touch of the oil of healing.

Many people will testify to the delight and healing properties of aromatic oils. They are intimate and tender and personal, just like Jesus was with people who were hurting. We are sometimes inclined to go wading in among people's wounds with a kind of clinical precision – like a surgeon with a knife. We are scared to be tender, although we wouldn't like to admit it. But these deep wounds need oil, not knives. We have had the cuts, now we need to be gentle and let the body heal itself. Most healing is about letting the body, with its own innate tendency to wholeness, heal itself. We just need to tend it, allow it that space and that time. Part of that tending involves lots of prayer, deep attentiveness to the suffering of the other, but also to their giftedness.

The same innate urge to wholeness is working in what Jesus said about healing. He did not equate wholeness with perfection; he was much less worried than his disciples about conformity to *'our group'*. In effect, he said that the movement of the Holy Spirit has its own power, which, when called upon, will be stronger than any other.

But to be agents of the Spirit in the world, we don't just need the oil of healing. We need what Jesus called the salt of friendship. Salt in a wound is not like oil. It stings, it smarts – and yet we know it is good; like a trusted friend who can say the things to us that we need to hear. To confront the challenges of justice as healing is not easy or comfortable. It may involve us in taking risks, risking unpopularity, disapproval even. It stings to go beyond our own jagged boundaries with their own pain. It is hard work to haul the boulders of our self-interest away from where they sit midstream, blocking the flow of the Spirit. Above all, it stings when we draw attention to the places where people are suffering under the cover of silence and and invisibility.

The Japanese theologian Kosuke Koyama has written: *What is love if it remains invisible and intangible? Those who do not love a brother or sister whom they have seen cannot love God whom they have not seen. The devastating poverty in which millions of children live is visible. Racism is visible. Machine guns are visible. Slums are visible. The gap between rich and poor is glaringly visible. Our response to these realities must be visible. Grace cannot function in a world of invisibility. Yet in our world, the rulers try to make invisible the alien, the orphan, the hungry and thirsty, the sick and imprisoned. This is violence. Their bodies must remain visible. There is a connection between invisibility and violence. People, because of the image of God they embody, must remain seen. Faith, hope and love are not vital except in what is seen. Religion seems to raise up the invisible and despise what is visible. But it is the 'see, hear, touch' gospel of Jesus that can nurture the hope which is free from deception.*

The impetus to do this hard and often unpopular work does not come from theories, or 'thou shalts'. It comes, like the urge to friendship, from our desire for what is lively, vivid, life-enhancing, for freedom and laughter, for all the things we give and receive in friendship. Perhaps we should look and hope most for the savour and seasoning of friendship in our life as churches together, in our sharing of the good news in the world, should see others first as potential friends rather than as the raw material for ecclesiastical negotiation or religious persuasion. There are many ways in which we are different – we are, after all, a body with different limbs – and so many ways in which we can be divided. Only the urge to love, which is a gift of the Holy Spirit, is strong enough to hold it all together.

So I believe that, as individuals and churches and denominations, we need to seek *to re-present the best vision and values of our various traditions*. We don't always know about the best of each other. Indeed, we don't even always know the best about ourselves, and sharing can help us learn both.

And we need to engage in *a committed and respectful dialogue of equals*, which seeks to affirm our common ground (of which there is actually a great deal), to dispel ignorance and sectarianism, to struggle honestly with significant areas of difference and to build relationships of friendship in which the memory of past divisions can begin to be healed by a mutual hope for the future.

And we need to practise *voluntary self-limitation*, in order to model the kind of political and cultural exchanges and possibilities we might hope for ourselves and therefore expect from others; whether that is self-limitation in consumerism, in cultural and spiritual imperialism or in forced or manipulated proselytism.

Such practices cannot simply be imposed; they require to be from the ground up as well as from the top down. And in all of them, Christians can learn from the justice and peace makers of other faiths, and from artists, ecologists and community activists among others.

What the Lord requires of us

Greeting

Blessed is our God always, now and for ever and to the ages of ages.
AMEN

Opening responses

O Lord, open our lips,
AND OUR MOUTHS WILL DECLARE YOUR PRAISE.
Create in us a clean heart, O God,
AND PUT A NEW AND RIGHT SPIRIT WITHIN US.
Do not cast us away from your presence,
AND DO NOT TAKE YOUR HOLY SPIRIT FROM US.
Restore to us the joy of your salvation,
AND SUSTAIN IN US A WILLING SPIRIT. *(Psalm 51:15, 10–12)*

Song   *Inspired by love and anger   (Common Ground)*

Prayers of approach and confession

These are the words of the Lord: Stop at the crossroads; look for the ancient paths; ask, 'Where is the way that leads to what is good?' Then take that way and you will find peace. But they said, 'We will not.'

Eternal God, Creator
You have spoken through your prophets to show us what is good
that we should act justly, love mercy, walk humbly with you upon the earth. But of ourselves we are not just, we are not merciful, we are not humble. Children die in fear, neighbour makes war with neighbour, the earth itself groans and cracks under the weight of our conflicts.
Of ourselves we are not just, we are not merciful, we are not humble.
KYRIE ELEISON, KYRIE ELEISON, KYRIE ELEISON

We bear the weight of our own chaos, within us and around us
We have sought to deny our humanness
We have broken down your ordering
We have made idols of our small knowledge

and we do not know what we do not know.

Of ourselves we are not just, we are not merciful, we are not humble.

KYRIE ELEISON

Lamentations

(during these, a single repeating drumbeat can be sounded)

Voice 1:   All who pass by, look and see
is there any sorrow like my sorrow?

Voice 2:   Our property is in the hands of strangers;
foreigners are living in our homes
our fathers have been killed by the enemy
and now our mothers are widows
ALL WHO PASS BY, LOOK AND SEE
IS THERE ANY SORROW LIKE MY SORROW?

Voice 1:   Murderers roam through the country,
we risk our lives when we look for food
hunger has made us burn with fever
until our skin is as hot as an oven
ALL WHO PASS BY, LOOK AND SEE
IS THERE ANY SORROW LIKE MY SORROW?

Voice 2:   Our leaders have been taken and hanged
our old men are shown no respect
the old people no longer sit at the city gate
and the young people no longer make music
ALL WHO PASS BY, LOOK AND SEE
IS THERE ANY SORROW LIKE MY SORROW?

Voice 1:   Happiness has gone out of our lives;
grief has taken the place of our dances.
We are sick at our very hearts
and can hardly see through our tears
ALL WHO PASS BY, LOOK AND SEE
IS THERE ANY SORROW LIKE MY SORROW?

Voice 2:   We looked until we could look no longer
for help that never came.
We kept waiting for help
from a nation that had none to give
ALL WHO PASS BY, LOOK AND SEE
IS THERE ANY SORROW LIKE MY SORROW?

Voice 1:   Look at me Lord, the city cries;
see me in my misery
Why have you abandoned us so long?
Will you ever remember us again?
ALL WHO PASS BY, LOOK AND SEE
IS THERE ANY SORROW LIKE MY SORROW?

(the drum continues with its single beat, gradually dying away)

Silence

(out of the silence, a solo voice sings the first verse of the song)

Song   *This is my song   (Tune: Finlandia)*
This is my song, O God of all the nations   *(solo)*
A song of peace, for your land and for mine.
This is my home, the country where my heart is.
Here grew my hopes and dreams for humankind.
But other hearts in other lands are beating.
And dreams are everywhere as true as mine.

MY COUNTRY'S SKIES ARE BLUER THAN THE OCEAN   *(ALL)*
AND SUNLIGHT SHINES ON CLOVERLEAF AND PINE
BUT OTHER LANDS HAVE SUNLIGHT TOO AND CLOVER
AND SKIES ARE EVERYWHERE AS BLUE AS MINE
O HEAR MY SONG, O GOD OF ALL THE NATIONS
A SONG OF PEACE, FOR YOUR LAND AND FOR MINE.

Words of assurance

Reader: You, my child, will be called a prophet of the Most High God.
You will go ahead of the Lord to prepare his road for him,

to tell his people that they will be saved by having their sins forgiven.

Our God is merciful and tender. He will cause the bright dawn of salvation to rise on us, and to shine from heaven on all those who live in the dark shadow of death, to guide our steps into the paths of peace.
AND WE, MORTAL THOUGH WE ARE,
WILL REST ASSURED IN HOPE
BECAUSE YOU WILL NOT ABANDON US
IN THE WORLD OF THE DEAD.
YOU HAVE SHOWN US THE PATHS THAT LEAD TO LIFE
AND YOUR PRESENCE WILL FILL US WITH JOY

Sharing the Word

Reader: Micah 6:6–8

Then, those gathered are invited to turn into small groups of three or four and spend a few minutes sharing thoughts about how each one sees the possibility of doing justice, or loving mercy or walking humbly with God in their own situation.

Symbolic action

Leader: In this place, the painful insights of the past, and the awesome hopes and demands of the future converge in the decisions and actions of the present.

(Around the room/hall/church are three stations at which different things may be done)

At the place for justice, there is a large map of the world and some small votive candles. You are invited to light a candle and place it as a prayer and an intention for action for somewhere which is crying out for justice…

At the place for mercy, there are paper and pens. You are invited to write a short letter to someone you need to say a word to, or who needs to hear a word from you…perhaps someone who needs people to stand beside them…

At the place for humility, there is a bowl of earth. The word 'humility' comes from the word for earth. You are invited to hold some soil in your hand, and reflect on a way in which you can tread more lightly on the earth, to conserve it and to value it

(As this is being done, music can be played, or short songs can be sung)

Song   *I bind unto myself today*

Prayers of intercession
Jesus Christ, Redeemer
You became like us
that we, unpromising raw material as we are,
might be saved from despair
might grow in love to be more like you.
It is your promise and our hope.
So we pray for a world mad with violence,
for countries and continents facing extraordinary challenges
for individuals hurt or distressed.
They are so many.
Christ be beside them, Christ be within them
LORD IN YOUR MERCY, HEAR OUR PRAYER

That we might act justly
judging as we would be judged,
ready to lay aside our own prejudices
for the sake of a world, country, community
in which being human matters most
we pray, O Christ,
and we remember everyone who, in these last days
has suffered violence, insult or injury
for their ethnicity, their religion, their gender, their sexual orientation
or just because they were in the wrong place at the wrong time.
They are so many.

Christ, be beside them, behind them, before them.
LORD IN YOUR MERCY, HEAR OUR PRAYER

That we might love mercy
that our own nation might be characterised
not first for the beauty of its landscape,
or the glories of its history
but for its kindness to strangers
its care for its weakest members
its solidarity with people living in want in other parts of the world
we pray, O Christ
and we remember everyone who, in these last days
has suffered fear, sickness, anxiety or bereavement.
They are so many.
Christ comfort and restore them.
LORD IN YOUR MERCY, HEAR OUR PRAYER

That we might walk humbly with you
in whose eternity empires come and go like leaves on the wind;
putting down pride of country, church or tradition
sensitive to your good creation and our bad stewardship
helping us to live within limits,
giving us a sense of proportion in all things
we pray, O Christ
and we remember everyone who, in these last days
has found themselves landless or uprooted,
whose land is poisoned or degraded or devastated
and those who have lost everything.
They are so many.
Christ be beneath them, above them, in quiet and in danger
LORD IN YOUR MERCY, HEAR OUR PRAYER

Holy Spirit, Sustainer,
in the confusion of our times,
you are our advocate, speaking to bring clarity.
In the anxious complexity of our hearts
you are our friend, inspiring us.

Look gently on our fondest dreams of peace
for our world
preserve us from cynicism
and sustain us in a living hope
not in our own strength but in your power to love
and to bring change to hopeless places.
So we pray, O Christ;
be in the hearts of all that love us
and in the mouths of friends and strangers,
today and always,
in the name of the Triune God,
Creator, Redeemer, Sustainer
AMEN

Affirmation
The Spirit of the Lord is upon me
HE HAS CHOSEN ME TO BRING GOOD NEWS TO THE POOR.
HE HAS SENT ME TO PROCLAIM LIBERTY TO THE CAPTIVES
AND RECOVERY OF SIGHT TO THE BLIND;
TO FREE THE OPPRESSED
AND ANNOUNCE THAT THE TIME HAS COME
WHEN THE LORD WILL SAVE HIS PEOPLE
This is the word of the Lord
THANKS BE TO GOD

Song (the people stand and join hands to sing)
STAND, O STAND FIRM
STAND, O STAND FIRM
STAND, O STAND FIRM
AND SEE WHAT THE LORD CAN DO

Blessing
O Lord Jesus, stretch forth your wounded hands in blessing
over your people,
to heal and to restore,
and to draw them to yourself and to one another in love
AMEN

Keeping the earth beautiful
A service of creation and healing

This service was prepared for use in Iona Abbey by a visiting school group.
The references can be changed to more appropriate local ones.

Opening responses
We are here to worship God
WE HAVE COME TO SING AND TO PRAY
We are happy to meet in the Abbey
THANK YOU FOR THE PERSON ON OUR LEFT
AND THE PERSON ON OUR RIGHT
We are seeing things on Iona
THAT WE WOULD NEVER DREAM OF SEEING AT HOME
Thank you God for loving us
THANK YOU FOR BEING HERE TONIGHT

Song *God's got the whole world in his hands*
1. God's got the whole world in his hands (x4)
2. He's got the kids of Bellahouston in his hands (x3)
   He's got the whole world in his hands
3. She's got the lambs and the sheep in her hands…
4. He's got the cliffs and the sky, the sand and the sea…
5. She's got the islands and the cities in her hands…
6. God's got everybody here in his hands…

Prayer of approach
You are our Maker, God.
You have given us a world full of wonder and beauty.
You have asked us to care for your world
and to care for each other.
You are our Maker
AND WE ARE GLAD

You are our friend, Jesus.
You tell us stories of seeds and of cities.
You confront us with joy and with justice.

You call us to life and to death and to new beginnings.
You are our friend
AND WE ARE GLAD

You are our wisdom, Holy Spirit.
You strengthen us and surprise us,
and you dance where you choose to.
You listen to our fears and you fill us with courage.
You are our wisdom
AND WE ARE GLAD

You love us, God.
You know us.
You know how we hurt ourselves
            how we hurt each other
            how we hurt your world.
We are sorry, God.
We want to change.
Help us and heal us.

Listen to God's words.
I love you.
I forgive you.
I ask you to act justly and to love kindly.
I call you to walk with me.
THANK YOU GOD.
AMEN

Psalm (a reworded version of Psalm 36:5–9)
God, your love is huge,
your loyalty reaches the skies,
your goodness is as high as the mountains
your fairness is as deep as the sea.
Every living thing,
from the biggest to the smallest,
the fastest to the slowest,
is in your care.

How excellent is your love –
we are sheltered in your house of security and happiness.

You give us food to share and we enjoy it;
you give us water when we are thirsty;
you are the beginning of all life
and because of your light, we know where we are going.

Song of Creation (e.g. Oh the Earth is the Lord's: Common Ground)

either
Drama: Seven Hard Days (see Resources)
If this is used, in each musical interlude a symbol can be carried through
the church and placed centrally, e.g. a candle, water (which can be liberally
sprinkled on the congregation en route), flowers and fruit, sun and moon
and stars symbols, a selection of cuddly toys!

or
Readings relating to creation (see Resources)

Prayers of thanksgiving and concern
God, we thank you that we are alive.
Thank you for the birds and the bees
and the sands and the seas,
for the moon that gives us light at night
and for the sun that gives us light all day.
Thank you for good food to eat,
for sherbet and sugar and salt and meat.
Thank you, God, for all that you've done.
AMEN

We pray tonight for refugees in Kosovo, *(change as appropriate)*
for people who are hungry and ill,
for people who have no warm clothes, no shoes to wear,
no clean water and no food.
Please be with everyone who is trying to help them.
Please bring peace to Kosovo and healing to your world.
AMEN

God, you have made the world beautiful
and sometimes we mess it up.
We want to keep your world beautiful.
Help us to keep it clean.
AMEN

Activity

People are invited to come and place a symbol of creation on a green cloth. Symbols could include leaves, stones, flowers, shells, etc. They are invited to do this as a sign of their intention to work to keep the world beautiful.

Closing responses

God, we have been learning about you
WE HAVE ENJOYED BEING HERE
Now it is time to leave the Abbey
BUT YOU WILL ALWAYS BE WITH US
Help us to go into the world
AND MAKE IT A BETTER PLACE.
AMEN

Song of Blessing   *(Common Ground)*

The peace of the earth be with you
the peace of the heavens too
the peace of the rivers be with you
the peace of the oceans too.
Deep peace falling over you,
God's peace growing in you

*(Psalms, prayers of thanksgiving and concern and responses –
Gary Graham, Lewis Mulligan, Tonia Pitman, Iona Smilie, Mark Grant,
Kiran Kaur, Andy McCulloch, all from Bellahouston Academy, Glasgow
Prayer of approach – Ruth Burgess)*

Where there is injury...
Hoping for healing in Northern Ireland

Duncan Morrow

Over thirty years, built on decades – even centuries – of experience, violence in Northern Ireland has taken on the shape of a circle moving through time. Each new scar is part of a chain which links every wound to its numerous predecessors and inevitable successors. At least that is how it looks to the academic or news reporter, observing how each victim is held to 'deserve' his or her fate because of the group label which attaches to him or her. Protestant fears Catholic fears Protestant. Republican kills loyalist kills republican. British hates Irish hates British.

Like all myths, this all-too-visible spiral carries its truth. And like all myths it too is built on simplification and exclusion. For Gerard had not killed anyone when they decided to shoot the first person to leave from evening mass that Sunday. John's company had sold some timber to the police when he was shot at point blank range as he got out of his car on his drive-way after another long day's work that dark, damp December night. And Tony was drunk and sitting alone eating the end of a carry-out pizza at 2 am when two drunken lads used sectarian hatred as grounds enough to kick and stab him and dump him in the river to drown. For all of them and their families there was no chain, only an unforeseen and devastating bolt from the blue. The marks they leave are no minor scars but wounds which shape the further course of life, sometimes to the point of paralysis. It is no longer a question of reminders, when old scars are remembered because of a strange damp feel in the air, but of a new and permanent climate. Waking up is reminder enough.

As every poet and novelist knows, war always leaves both a structured and a random legacy. Viewed at a distance, from the planners' room, a shape emerges which rationalises and understands the human costs. From the graveside, such a shape is less apparent. When the killing begins in earnest, the cry from the cemetery is 'Why me?' and the only honest answer from the community and its planners is 'Why not you?' And when conflict stumbles to an end without a clearcut winner, as has been our experience of the peace process, the unresolved whys of those who suffered without reason cannot be explained as heroic sacrifice for the victorious community. Nor even is their suffering drowned out by the deluge which follows a definitive defeat and at least allows a certain solidarity between the dead and injured and their unheroic compatriots.

Healing, the possibility of restoration to life, after such a complicated history must then also be both a complex and a simple experience. Political acts of reconciliation between community leaders, unprecedented gestures which build new hope, new histories of co-operation built over time in new and agreed institutions, a new confidence that justice can and will be done…all these are crucial elements if the spiral is to be arrested. But if the healing process is to restore us to health, it will also be something painstaking and nuanced and sometimes taking almost contradictory forms.

At its most public and political, healing is the experience of a present in which the historic spiral of violence at last seems distant, incredible and maybe even unthinkable. It is visible at all the points of 'normal' conflict where unexpected generosity transforms past antagonism. In such events and from these places, new stories can enter the weave of history. When political leaders who articulated distance and hatred voluntarily stand on unified platforms, when marchers and residents find a creative way beyond previous visceral disputes about traditional marches and when the police go about their business for one day taking for granted their standing within the whole community we can speak already of healing. Within such transformed relationships, even the past is hard to predict. Dignity and humanity have always been present in Northern Ireland too, but so often they have been submerged by the power of the spiral of violence which belittled their existence and allowed them to be labelled irrelevant.

Ritual acts of change, contrition and memorial – and all political acts are ultimately connected to ritual – contain their own power and authority. The smoking of the pipe of peace may seem far removed from Belfast but, in a suitably Irish form, ritual is a crucial bridge from here to a there worth going to. Even limited to the public sphere, the simplicity of healing can be overdone. Everyone looks for reconciliation between Ulster Protestant and Irish Catholic, but beyond that vortex are the wider and largely unacknowledged relationships of Britain and Ireland to one another, of which Northern Ireland is only a part, and the even longer antagonism between Catholicism and Protestantism not only on these islands but throughout Christendom, of which events in Northern Ireland have only been a particularly vicious offspring. Healing in Ireland is healing in these other relationships. The unhealed wounds of Ireland are reminders of the unspoken rivalries of others too, and of the part others can play in the healing of Ireland's wounds. Even more deeply hidden are the wounds of wars within nations. For people in Northern Ireland, the deepest fear has sometimes been of being left alone: the fear of Irish Catholics marooned on the wrong side of the border by partition and of Protestants who find themselves disposable, stranded by other Britons on the wrong side of history as the tide of empire recedes.

But, in some senses, all these political and formal levels are the simple parts of healing. Their importance lies in the signal that healing in its most complex sense can be approached with the consent of the public leadership. For some things cannot be ritualised, and some things which require healing have hardly even been spoken.

Conflict in a television age is a question of never missing a funeral. For thirty-odd years now, both Catholic and Protestant in Ireland have been attendants at a parade of private and public anguish. Most of us watched and felt both excitement and horror, the helplessness of comfort and the embarrassment of the voyeur who knows he or she is just that. Too often we used our own fascination to justify our fears, lashing out and bringing no remedy for the anguish except more anger. The chain from one funeral to the next was us. Our fears came to define not only what we feel and what we remember but who we are. Instead of freedom and release we watchers became the people or peoples of these solidarities born in trauma, nurturing the trauma as our own instead of beating a different path. At the funerals of others we saw ourselves clearly as victims, but too seldom did we see our sense of innocence and anger as the platform for the next turn of the screw.

The logic of this chain of victimhood is both compelling and catastrophic. For, in Northern Ireland now, it is clear that being communities built on victimhood is both our tragic predicament and a prison of our own making. When enough people have been brought into the circle, each of us making our competing claims on compassion and solidarity, then every violent action from every quarter is the action of a sinner justified. Too often, and naturally, we have sought the easiest way to peace: to be rid of the perpetrator. But in spirals and chains we are not only the victim of their last action against us but also the victim of our own last attack which fuelled their anger: we are always victims of ourselves too. While violence has made us all aware of our claim on the scars of the victim, we have been less willing to claim our share of the marks on the forehead of the murderers. Northern Ireland is full of Abels, not descendants of Cain. And those who have really suffered are too often left alone to grieve for the depth of their wounds – and the only hope we offer is more of the same.

Healing, here as elsewhere, comes and will come unevenly, partially and messily if it comes at all. For some, healing is possible in the strength of support which enables even the deepest wounds to be carried in a still-whole person. It comes for some in faith, in which even these traumas can be held and the contradictions they raise cast in another context. For Gordon Wilson, whose daughter was killed in the Enniskillen bomb of 1987, it began with his daughter's freedom in death allowing him to forgive her killers. For others it comes through chance relationships and unexpected new turns, when we find ourselves suddenly in a new world. But for many of us, healing only begins when we recognise our own complicity not only as victims but also as perpetrators, and we go at last to all those who suffered for us and ask to be received back. In some deep sense, those who died were the random victims of all of us who survived. And those who mourn, mourn for all of us. 'Blessed are those who mourn, for they shall be comforted,' said Jesus on the hillside. When the unending and tragic sadness for our loss and wounds becomes our resting place, we too might begin to find healing in each other's compassion.

The memory of brokenness

Purification of the memory

Ian M. Fraser

Pope John Paul dedicated the Jubilee year 2000 to repentance and renewal. During it he promulgated the report *The Church and the Mistakes of the Past*, which was three years in preparation by the Sacred Congregation for the Doctrine of the Faith. In place of previous insipid half-apologies (e.g. the Jews were hard done by, but it was not the church's fault) there has been more substance this time. In spite of some consternation on the part of the Curia, who protested that the report would undermine the foundations of the church's authority, the Pope has stood firm, believing that one thing needed today is a 'purification of the memory'.

Up for repentance were: the church's record of antisemitism; the atrocities of the Crusades; the crimes of the Inquisition; the religious wars; the failure to resist the Nazis (without mention of the role of Pope Pius XII); the treatment of Galileo; and 'violent evangelism' (it is time that these two words were put together – witness Argentinians' rejection of the word 'mission' in favour of 'cominando', walking together). Unexpectedly, the ceremony of repentance also confessed 'sins against the dignity of women and the unity of the human race'.

I was in Dublin when Tony Blair asked forgiveness of the Irish people for the way in which, when people starved to death in the famine, food was shipped out of the country. That made impact. We have more awareness of the need for healing or reconciling of memories – 'purification' as the Pope would put it – in our time. Form confession may be superficial, an attempt to get shot of the sins of the past without cost (and why speak of the church's *'mistakes'* when these are actually *sins*?). But, accompanied by real repentance and amendment of life, confession brings to the surface things which fester from past history and allows them to be dealt with.

The past, even the sinful past, can then become a resource for determining present priorities and policies. It can enable us to live more truly as we reject what is now seen to be sinful, and take hold afresh of what is constructive for the establishment of God's kingdom.

The purification of memory has two distinctive features in the Old Testament. First, we may act and react carelessly and thoughtlessly, a prey to our own emotions and fears: and second, we may act and react forgetting what the fear can teach us. Take racism.

First: 'I am the Lord your God.' We are not to take our cue for living from the emotions and fears which may well up within us when we encounter people of different ethnic groups, histories, cultures, whom we may consider to be strange or threatening. We are to take our cue from God, who is no respecter of persons and who 'loves the foreigner' *(Deut. 10:19)*. We are to remember that God is Lord, and keep that before us to guide our conduct. It is from God that we learn how to manage our relationships with different kinds of people. The foreigner is to be 'as a native-born among you' *(Lev. 19:34)* for those who acknowledge God.

Second: the chosen people knew what it was like when the boot was on the other foot. 'You shall not oppress a stranger, for you were strangers in the land of Egypt' *(Exodus 23:8, cf. 22:21)*. The memory can do more than register the past, as in a snapshot. The purified memory can draw the past into the present so that it becomes a vivid force, a creative force. When Jesus said, 'Do this in remembrance of me,' that remembrance made his presence and power real for all who participate in faith in the action of the Lord's Supper.

As members and associates of the Iona Community, we use a 'book of remembrance' (in which each one is named on a particular day of the month, so that the Community may pray for those named on that day). The act of remembering one another before God is a means of sustaining one another in each day that passes. Other events and people claim our time and attention – quite properly so. But there comes a time when we focus on this one and that one, hold their lives up to God. That remembrance is life-giving.

The memory of brokenness and the hope of healing
A Communion liturgy

Gathering together in Christ's name

Call to worship

God of the past who has fathered us and mothered us
WE ARE HERE TO THANK YOU
God of the future who is always ahead of us
WE ARE HERE TO TRUST YOU
God of the present here in the midst of us
WE ARE HERE TO PRAISE YOU
God of life beyond us within us
WE CELEBRATE YOUR LOVE

Song *Take this moment (Common Ground)*

The memory of brokenness

Reader 1:   He went to a country far away…and spent everything he had… He was left without a thing. *(Luke 15:13–14)*

Prayers of approach and confession

Beloved God,
with the eagerness of a child, you wait for our coming,
with the urgency of a lover, you long for our return
with the anxious heart of a parent, your arms ache to hold us
and we who would come, restless or reluctant,
weary or wary,
hurting and yet hoping beyond hope
stand still, undecided.
We are drawn by the promise of your kindness
but we are afraid of your disappointment
of your judgement
of your turning away from us.

So many people have let us down
failed to deliver
refused us as we really are.
Are you one more shattered hope?
No one could blame you if you closed your door,
for we too have been the failures, the betrayers, the deniers,
we too have hurt, and hurt and hurt again.

Give us a moment, God, to face our fears and failures,
a moment to admit our need of your love…
(Silence)
LORD HAVE MERCY ON US
CHRIST HAVE MERCY ON US
LORD HAVE MERCY ON US
(or sung Kyrie)

Oh beloved God,
you are still there, still eager,
still waiting patiently with arms wide open.
The disappointment, the judgement, the turning away,
that's us, not you.
Forgive us and heal us
of all in us that recoils from our common humanity –
all pride, all fear,
all disgust, all shame;
you have given us such worth,
help us to take all creation at your valuation
and to know ourselves precious and loved.

We're coming home to you.
AMEN

God speaks

Reader 2: But while he was still far off, his father saw him and was
filled with compassion; he ran and put his arms round him
and kissed him. *(Luke 15:20)*

Gospel Luke 15:11–32

Sung *Alleluia (Common Ground)*

Reflections on the Word *(optional)*

Celebrating the Word made flesh
Reader1: The father called his servants… 'Let us celebrate with a feast! For this son of mine was dead but now is alive; was lost but now has been found.' And so the feasting began. *(Luke 15:22–24)*

Invitation
Celebrant: This is the invitation to a feast. God who has run out to meet us in Jesus, when we were still a long way off, is preparing a table for us right now. For we have come home, and God is full of wild rejoicing. To those who have come from far away, unsure of their reception, and to those who are always here, I say in the name of Christ, all are welcome at the table of the Lord. God has invited us, and turns no one away empty. Here, we are no longer strangers:

'THOSE IN WHOM WEALTH ABOUNDS WILL POOR AND HUNGRY BE, BUT THOSE WHO WOULD EAGERLY SEEK THE LORD SHALL NEVER BE IN WANT OF ANY BLESSING.'

Communion song *Amazing grace* or
Bread is blessed and broken (Common Ground)

The story
Reader: It was the night he was betrayed. Jesus was eating a meal with his friends. He took a piece of bread, gave thanks to God and said, 'This is my body, which is broken for you. Do this to remember me.' And he gave it to them. Later, after they had eaten, he took a cup of wine and said, 'This cup is God's new relationship with us, made possible by my death. Whenever you drink it, do it remembering me.'

Celebrant: As the lovers of Jesus have always done,
we do now as he did.
We set your gifts of bread and wine upon our table.
In them, you have promised to be with us.
Through them, we will remember you and you will heal us.
Let us give thanks.

Great prayer
The Lord be with you
AND ALSO WITH YOU
Lift up your hearts
WE LIFT THEM TO THE LORD
Let us give thanks to God
IT IS RIGHT TO GIVE OUR THANKS AND PRAISE

Lord Jesus, it's so good to know
that you really lived in the flesh,
walked where we walk, felt what we feel,
got tired, had sore and dirty feet,
needed to eat, and to think about
where the next meal was coming from.

But it's even better to know
that you enjoyed your food,
the scent of the perfume on your skin,
the wind on your face, a child in your arms
and the good wine at the wedding.
You didn't mind when people touched you,
even those who were thought of as unclean.
You kissed people with diseases
and leaned on your friend's shoulder.
Thank you for understanding our bodily pains and pleasures
and for valuing them.

Most of all, we thank you that for us,
for all of us,
you became homeless,

took on our brokenness and shame
and even our death
to open a way home for us
and offer us welcome, forgiveness, healing, love.
Here, now, you meet us and feed us.
In the company of all your friends,
how can we keep from singing.

Sung *Santo, santo, santo   (Common Ground)*

Holy Spirit, Spirit of the living God,
you breathe in us, on all that is inadequate and fragile.
You make living water spring even from our hurts themselves.
And, through you, the valley of fears becomes a place of wellsprings.
So, in an inner life with neither beginning nor end,
your continual presence makes new freshness break through.
(Sri Lanka)

…breathe now in us with justice on all that diminishes
or destroys God's children or God's creation…
…breathe now in us with peace to close the hostile distances
between people and nations…
…breathe now in us with protection for those bruised
by grinding indifference or the cruelty of others…
…breathe now in us with healing for those haunted
by the memory of suffering or shame…
…breathe now in us with love for those who are full of self-loathing,
who cannot love themselves or others…

Spirit of Jesus, come swiftly,
breathe in us, and on these gifts of bread and wine,
that sharing your blessing and your broken, risen life,
we may share your continual presence and reality,
and together, as your body,
live at home in your love
till no one is homeless.
We pray in your name with confidence…

Lord's prayer

We have bread, the bread of life
WE BREAK IT TO SHARE IT
We have wine, the cup of blessing
IT IS POURED OUT SO WE MAY DRINK
Here is the body and blood of our Lord
broken and poured out for us
IT IS THE NEW RELATIONSHIP FOR US
The bread we share is one
THOUGH WE ARE MANY, WE ARE ONE BODY
LET THERE BE PLENTY FOR EVERYONE, EVERYWHERE

Sharing the bread and wine

Sung   *Behold the lamb of God   (Common Ground)*

Sharing the Peace

Reader 2:   You are always here with me, and everything I have is
yours. But we have to celebrate and be glad, because the
one who was lost is now found.

Celebrant: The peace of the Lord Jesus Christ be with us all.

Prayer
Our brother Jesus,
we have shared your celebration
and you have refreshed us with love.
Now you set our feet upon the way,
and sometimes where you lead
we do not like or understand.
Walk beside us
until we find that on the road
is where you are
and where you are is going home.
BLESS US, LEAD US, LOVE US

AND BRING US HOME,
BEARING THE GOSPEL OF LIFE.
AMEN

Song *Mayenziwe   (Common Ground)*

Making the Good News accessible

Larry Nugent

AIDAC (Activists In Disability And Caring) is a multifaith-based consultative, negotiative and campaigning initiative, operated locally by post and the internet, so that disabled individuals can develop access and quality of life for all, by prayer, liturgy, writing, and lobbying the appropriate churches, local, regional, national, and world authorities.

Present building structures are based on the premise that all God's people should meet regularly and worship. But they are not designed to include disabled people. We need to depart from accepting church structures that are inaccessible or of limited access, and that make overwhelming demands on ourselves, our families, our carers, and our precious time.

We have a lot to learn from the early Celtic Church on openness and oneness with nature, when the community's places of worship were outside. Whether intentional or not, it was a true beginning to a physically barrier-free service, and when it was required to be inside, the house was the altar. The Good News was more accessible then than now.

Surely there must be more than the churches just taking note and giving out sympathy; they must change the hostile environment that they control, that confronts and dehumanises the many disabled people in God's creation. We do not want tea and buns or sympathy. We want to be able to break and share bread and drink from the cup, whenever and wherever we congregate with other believers.

AIDAC is a touching place, giving out updated information that will help those concerned for disability and caring. It makes no demands and seeks no commitments. At most it is only a signpost. It is how we develop and link up spiritual practice with constructive action that will make our places of worship accessible and barrier-free.

Community and inclusion are important to all of us, and prayer, in thought, word, and action, is often our everyday tool and enabler. To quote Lord George MacLeod, the founder of the Iona Community, 'Worship is not a once a week event, it should take different forms as we dwell too much on the spiritual and not enough on the physical.'

From the three annual programme events on Ability and Disability that have taken place at the MacLeod Centre on Iona, it is apparent that what is needed is a genuine commitment by all churches to eradicate the 'not enough on the physical' when it comes to sharing worship with the elderly frail, the chronically sick and disabled people.

AIDAC itself takes on the mantle of intercessor, at least for individuals. At the moment local churches are not involved so it would be wrong and misguided to assume their blessing. It is hoped that we can become a recognised central point to intercede on behalf of the individual in areas related to access the whole year round, in a way that will keep pilgrims in contact with progress.

It is important that all who wish have the chance to enjoy worship in a barrier-free environment, and to know spiritual and physical inclusion and community. The words of the ancient Celtic blessing are an appropriate prayer.

The blessing of St Patrick's breastplate
Christ be with me, Christ be within me,
Christ behind me, Christ before me,
Christ beside me, Christ to win me,
Christ to comfort and restore me,
Christ beneath me, Christ above me,
Christ in quiet, Christ in danger,
Christ in hearts of all that love me,
Christ in mouth of friend and stranger.

Images of naked feeling

Joyce Gunn Cairns

I remember in my youth I had a list of six things I most loathed about my face and body. Top of the list was my hair. It was the most terrible curse to have fine hair in the sixties, when what one longed for most of all was thick, wiry hair that would stay in place like a brick, with the aid of back-combing and lacquer. My sister had – of course – thick, wiry hair, and was renowned for her talent in hairstyling (which occupation excluded every-one else from the bathroom for at least two hours in the morning). Many women who have a sister will acknowledge, if they dare, the ambivalent feelings experienced in this most central of relationships, the bond of love and admiration on the one hand, and the torment of jealousy on the other. I was always so intent on my sister's gifts and beauty, and my comparable inadequacy; the rest of the world was a mere blur.

I had a boyfriend when I was fourteen who was tall and handsome, and he took me out to 'the picters'. The whole *raison d'être* of going to the cinema was to have a 'necking session' of course; the film was entirely irrelevant. Although he fancied me when we set out (I think!), when we emerged I had streaky pan stick on my face, my mouth was red raw, my mascara was all over the place, and my hair was plastered flat to one side of my head. That was the end of him! I never stopped to think that he might be inter-ested in my brain. What good was a brain, after all, when one was such a freak?

I can laugh now at the memory of this list – fine hair, small low-slung breasts, thick ankles, eczema, narrow sloping shoulders, hooded eyes(!) – but these unhappy features, real or imagined, were the focus for deep-seated feelings of loathing which plagued me all my days, and I cursed and cursed them like a mantra through years of often suicidal depression.

At the time of writing this I can say I have experienced much healing. I am able to laugh at myself more readily, and that is a great blessing. Another list of six, this time sources of healing, would be my two wonderful sons, seven years in therapy, my vocation as an artist, sexual pleasure, prayer and last but not least, friends.

I cannot say in simple outline what kind of images I create as an artist, because to do so is to attempt to pinpoint in clear-cut categories a process which is, of necessity, fluid. It is true to say, however, that a large part of the body of my work over the years has been self-portraits; that is to say that I have expressed my strong sense of vocation through equally strong images of my body. In this way I have become more reconciled to my body, and so to the world around me. To put it differently: as I paint my face and body, I am simultaneously (though not consciously) acknowledging its existence and thus its validity. As a result I am freer (free*er*, not free) from a fixation on my ugliness (spiritual/emotional/physical), more open and responsive to others and to the environment. People have often said things like, 'That disnae look anything like ye,' or, 'You don't do yourself justice.' But those who can find in my work a parallel with their own struggle to free their beautiful creative Self never make any such comment.

In the last two years I have enjoyed a lot of recognition as an artist, and this has confirmed me in my sense of my work as a God-given vocation, a source of healing for myself and others who have found in it a reflection of their own raw humanity. Recently I sold a painting in the Royal Scottish Academy in Edinburgh, and the person who bought it said that the emotion he experienced in relation to it resonated with the emotion he recalled when he saw the Goya paintings in the Prado in Madrid, those from the artist's dark period. (He was speaking of a comparable soul quality, and not of course of any comparable technical ability). I felt both affirmed and unnerved by this comment. Goya confronted the dark chasms of his mind to a terrifying degree, and paid a terrible price. Does such a price have to be paid before one can touch the exquisite depths of one's own creativity? The question remains open: Is there an invariable link between the trauma (such as I suffered as a child) which gives rise to painful memories, and the impulse/ability to give expression to one's creative potential? Is the expression of one's creative gifts no more nor less than a longing for healing of those painful memories?

Healing the memory

Sylvia Pearson

It is sixty-three years since the first rape when I was three. It happened again when I was five, and again when I was a mature woman of thirty-six.

The first rape was perpetrated by a stranger, a young man from the local sawmill who had sawdust in his crinkly red hair and in the creases of his leather shoes. I did not understand what was happening to me. I felt awful fear and pain. I thought I had been split up the middle. As in most cases of child rape, I believed him – that he had the power to search me out *anywhere* if I dared to tell anyone. I hid for hours in a backgreen coal bunker until a neighbour discovered me. My dress, clean on that day, my pants and socks were stiff with blood – and something else, a thick substance which had a smell. She was drunk but kindly, washed me and my clothes, and then took me by the hand to my mother, pleading that I had been playing hide-and-seek, and not to punish me. I think she guessed the truth but, as far as I know, did not share it with my mother.

The second incident involved the breaking of my trust because the man was a courtesy uncle of a friend. He lured me with chocolate, a luxury in those war years. Again there was fear and pain – and shame, followed by the agonising inability to tell. This man's skill and patience in 'preparing' me were such that I did not suspect his intentions until it was too late. By the time the red light blazed he had me tied to his bed in an attic room. An extra legacy from this was a feeling of guilt, of self-disgust.

At thirty-six I was taken totally by surprise and knocked unconscious. This time I informed the police, and was deeply humiliated for my efforts. 'Had I been wearing something titillating at the time?' was the first question put to me. My anger and longing for revenge were boundless. By then, I was more enlightened by press coverage of this type of crime, but the guilt and self-loathing persisted.

It was only when an elderly friend confided that she did not know why I was not totally unhinged and bitter and twisted by my experiences that I realised for the first time that there had indeed been some kind of healing. We discussed it, and her gentle questioning led me to recall my 'good witnesses', people who had found out about these shameful happenings.

An infant-Sunday-School teacher, perceptive and observant, had evidently cared enough to read the signals I was sending out. I look back now and recognise the subtle ways in which she affirmed me with a huge injection of love. All this she did while battling with cancer, although I did not know this at the time. She gave me her Bible, a slim, leather-covered book with gold-edged pages, her initials embossed on the front. It smelled of lavender, her smell, and became a treasured possession. I was bereft when she died so soon after our special times together when she kept me behind after Sunday School, and read and sang and talked to me. I am forever in her debt.

Of course, my very good witness was she who had initially touched on the subject of these traumas. But for her, I would never have lowered the net and trawled up those memories from the depths, would never have been able to experience the revelations of healing which continued to come through friends and associates. Those people, through their encouragement and love, enabled and strengthened me.

When I started to write creatively, it became clear that here was a way to benefit from a type of self-help. Teachers and other writers inspired my trust. Gradually, painfully, I began to record events. Tears choked me as I met the final test of reading aloud my own words. After years of reliving those times through committing them to paper, the cutting edge of my writings lost some of its lethal sharpness.

Until a couple of years ago, there had been one sticking point which constantly plunged me into a morass of despair and doubt as to whether I would *ever* 'recover' in the way which I regarded as the pinnacle of achievement. It was this. Having watched documentaries and read articles about 'forgiving and forgetting', I had concluded that I could forget, but forgive? Never! Convincing psychotherapists seemed to indicate that *both* were necessary for full, lasting healing. I simply did not have it in me to pardon what those rapists had done to me. And then one blessed, Christ-centred friend, a woman the same age as myself, summed it all up for me in one sentence. She said, 'It's not for you to forgive, Sylvia; leave that to a higher power.' Relieved of this onerous responsibility, I was plucked from that barbed hook. I bless that wise woman.

The pain eased. The acid of resentment became alkaline. It was not a smooth journey. There were many trips and falls along the way, but through patient insistence that I could be in no way to blame, had never invited the rapes, and was now a 'clean' worthwhile woman who would eventually feel able to shed a legacy of suspicion and bitterness, I recovered and became a survivor rather than a victim – which I had thus far felt myself to be.

Thirty years ago I would never have believed this possible. Not everyone in a like situation has had the benefit of the only real treatment for this kind of abuse – love. My heart goes out to them. I am so fortunate to have known the nurturing of those few people. They have, through their gift of love, at a time when I felt so utterly *un*lovable, healed the memory.

Made in God's image

This liturgy was first used in worship remembering and praying for healing for women and children across the world who suffer violence and exclusion, and for the many men who also share that suffering. It is best (though not essential) that the worshipping community be seated in a circle or semi-circle. In a central and visible place, a big mirror should be placed, with a large candle and many small votive lights in front of it. Four readers will be needed for the parts indicated. The leadership of the rest of the order (those parts in normal, lower case type) may be shared.

Four pieces of black or dark cloth will also be needed to drape over the mirror.

Call to worship
Beloved God, Source of all that is
IN YOU WE LIVE AND MOVE AND HAVE OUR BEING
Jesus Emmanuel, God with us
WITH YOU, WE WALK THE WAY OF LOVE
Creator Spirit, fire of our lives
THROUGH YOU WE ARE MADE ONE
God, Trinity of love, community of life
WE ARE MADE IN YOUR IMAGE
We are many, and we are one
WE ARE MADE IN YOUR IMAGE
OUR HEARTS SEEK YOUR FACE
AND WE PRAISE YOU

Song *Sing for God's glory (Common Ground)*

The glory of the face of God
Voice 1:   This evening, you will know that it was the Lord who brought you out of Egypt. In the morning you will see the dazzling light of the Lord's presence.
(Ex. 16:6–7)

Voice 2:   When Moses had finished speaking to them, he covered his face with a veil.

Whenever Moses went into the tent of the Lord's presence to speak to the Lord, he took the veil off. When he came out, he would tell the people of Israel everything that he had been commanded to say, and they would see that his face was shining. *(Ex. 34:33–35)*

Song *Peruvian Gloria*   *(Common Ground)*

The image, distorted

Reader 1:   The number of men who ate was about five thousand, not counting the women and children. *(Matt.14:21)*
FOR NOW WE SEE IN A MIRROR, DARKLY

(Reader then drapes a piece of black cloth over a corner of the mirror)

Reader 2:   So the Levite took his concubine and put her outside with the men. They raped her and abused her all night long and didn't stop until morning… When her husband opened the door to go on his way, he found his concubine lying in front of the house with her hands reaching for the door. He said, 'Get up. Let's go.' But there was no answer… Then he took his concubine's body, cut it into twelve pieces, and sent one piece to each of the twelve tribes of Israel. *(Judges 19)*
FOR NOW WE SEE IN A MIRROR, DARKLY

(Reader drapes a piece of black cloth over another corner of the mirror)

Reader 3:   The woman was a Gentile, born in the region of Phoenicia in Syria. She begged Jesus to drive the demon out of her daughter. But Jesus answered, 'Let us first feed the children. It isn't right to take the children's food and throw it to the dogs.' 'Sir,' she answered, 'even the dogs under the table eat the children's leftovers!' *(Mark 7:26–28)*
FOR NOW WE SEE IN A MIRROR, DARKLY

(Reader drapes a piece of black cloth over the top of the mirror)

Reader 4: Jesus' disciples returned, and they were greatly surprised to find him talking to a woman. *(John 4:27)*
FOR NOW WE SEE IN A MIRROR, DARKLY

(Reader drapes a piece of black cloth along the bottom of the mirror, which is now partially covered, but not completely obscured)

Silence

Prayer
Our brother Jesus,
For the suffering of the millions of women and children
who are still not counted in the profit and loss accounts of the world
whose poverty feeds the banks and the appetites of the rich
forgive us
FOR THE WOUND OF THE DAUGHTER OF MY PEOPLE WOUNDS ME TOO

For the suffering of the millions of women and children
who are still raped, abused and killed
in the waging of wars, and in their own homes
forgive us
FOR THE WOUND OF THE DAUGHTER OF MY PEOPLE WOUNDS ME TOO

For the suffering of the millions of women and children
who are still insulted, discriminated against, marginalised
because of their race, their difference, their otherness
forgive us
FOR THE WOUND OF THE DAUGHTER OF MY PEOPLE WOUNDS ME TOO

For the suffering of the millions of women and children
who are still denied full personhood
equal opportunity, exercise of all their gifts, even in your church
forgive us
FOR THE WOUND OF THE DAUGHTER OF MY PEOPLE WOUNDS ME TOO

For the suffering of all the men who have learned the hard way,
through poverty, sexual violence, racism, homophobia, exclusion,
what life is like for most women in the world
For the broken lives, broken community, broken image
forgive us

Sung *Kyrie eleison   (Common Ground)*

WE TURN TO CHRIST
WE REPENT OF OUR SINS
WE RENOUNCE EVIL
Jesus said, 'Let the children come to me; do not stop them;
theirs is the kingdom of God'
AND HE BLESSED THEM

Jesus said, 'Whoever is without sin, throw the first stone'
AND THEY ALL WENT AWAY

Jesus said, 'Because of that answer,
what you want will be done for you'
AND HER DAUGHTER WAS HEALED

Jesus said, 'Give me a drink'
AND MANY BELIEVED BECAUSE OF THE WOMAN

Jesus our brother, help us to start believing again,
accepting with joy our whole humanity made in your image
THROUGH CHRIST OUR LORD, AMEN.

*(During each saying of Jesus, one of the pieces of black cloth is removed
from the mirror, till by the end it is completely uncovered)*

Christ the image of the unseen God
Voice 1:   Six days later, Jesus took with him Peter and the brothers
James and John and led them up a high mountain where
they were alone. As they looked on, a change came over
Jesus; his face was shining like the sun, and his clothes were

dazzling white… While he was talking, a shining cloud came over them, and a voice from the cloud said, 'This is my own dear Son, with whom I am pleased – listen to him.'

(The large candle in front of the mirror is lit)

Voice 2:   Your word in our lives, eternal
becomes the mirror where we see
the true reflection of ourselves –
children and image of God

Song *Loving Spirit, loving Spirit (Common Ground)*

During the singing of this song, people are invited to come forward and light a votive candle from the large one, as a sign of prayer for some person or group known or of concern to you in whom the image of God has been denied. (The song may be sung twice if necessary to allow enough time.)

The Spirit in each for the good of all

Voice 3:   What we see now is like a dim image in a mirror; then we shall see face to face. What I know now is only partial; then it will be complete, as complete as God's knowledge of me. Meanwhile, these three things remain: faith, hope and love; and the greatest of these is love. *(1 Cor.13:12–13)*

Voice 4:   Then it was as if I suddenly saw the secret beauty of their hearts, the depths of their hearts, where neither sin nor desire nor self-knowledge can reach, the core of their reality, the person that each one is in God's eyes. If only they could see themselves as they really are. If only we could see each other that way all the time, there would be no more war, no more hatred, no more cruelty, no more greed… I suppose the big problem would be that we would fall down and worship each other. *(Thomas Merton)*

Prayer

O Living God,
For your good creation,
for the beautiful workings of our bodies
for your image deep within us
for your presence strong among us
we give thanks, and we pray.
For now we see in a mirror, darkly
BUT THEN WE SHALL SEE FACE TO FACE

O Jesus our Saviour,
For your sharing of our life,
for your calling of us as your friends
for your cherishing of us in our brokenness
for your inviting us to follow you in the fullness of our humanity
we give thanks, and we pray
For now we see in a mirror, darkly
BUT THEN WE SHALL SEE FACE TO FACE

O Spirit of grace and truth,
for revealing yourself in community
for laying bare the grievous wounds of oppression and injustice
for bringing us healing through the work of justice and mercy
for inspiring us and firing us with courage to change
we give thanks, and we pray
For now we see in a mirror, darkly
BUT THEN WE SHALL SEE FACE TO FACE

O Trinity of life,
For the company of faithful people,
for the work and witness of many across the world,
and for the ones known and dear to us,
who have lived, and who have died
showing the face of God to others,
because they trusted in a whole body
and a common humanity
and the unity of God,
we give thanks, and we pray

For now we see in a mirror, darkly
BUT THEN WE SHALL SEE FACE TO FACE

As your daughters and sons,
may we be brought nearer to the image and vision of your love
THROUGH THE GRACE OF THE HOLY SPIRIT. AMEN

Sharing a blessing

Voice 1:   We are all now invited to stand and look at the faces of the people around us, to see in each other the image of God, and to bless one another in sung words from the scriptures.

Voice 2:   Some saw the Baptist, some saw Elijah, others a prophet from long ago, but may we see in each other the Christ of today.

Sung   *May the Lord   (Common Ground)*
May the Lord, mighty God
bless and keep you for ever;
grant you peace, perfect peace,
courage in every endeavour.

Lift up your eyes and see God's face
and God's grace for ever;
may the Lord, mighty God,
bless and keep you for ever.

Closing prayer

O God, you have made us for yourself,
and against your longing there is no defence.
Mark us with your love,
and release in us a passion for your justice
in our disfigured world;
that we may turn from our guilt and face you
our heart's desire.
AND THE GRACE OF THE LORD JESUS CHRIST
THE LOVE OF GOD
AND THE COMMUNION OF THE HOLY SPIRIT
BE WITH US ALL. AMEN

Praying for the dawn

Keeping on keeping on
An order of prayer for people with chronic illness

Opening words
Our faith is in God, our Maker
KNOWN IN CREATION
REVEALED IN SCRIPTURE
EXPERIENCED WITHIN

Our trust is in Jesus, our Redeemer
KNOWN THROUGH HIS BODY
REVEALED IN SCRIPTURE
EXPERIENCED WITHIN

Our life is in the Spirit, our Sustainer
KNOWN IN HISTORY
REVEALED IN SCRIPTURE
EXPERIENCED WITHIN

A prayer
God, Creator and Lover,
you see everything you have made,
and all you have made is good.
Your goodness is at the centre of our lives,
reaching out to you,
creating wholeness within
Sung IN THE LORD IS MY TRUE SALVATION… *(Taizé)*

Jesus, Redeemer and Friend,
You came to share the brokenness
of our world and of our lives:
and through your love
that brokenness is transformed for ever
by the cross and the empty tomb
IN THE LORD IS MY TRUE SALVATION…

Holy Spirit, Sustainer,
Your Pentecostal flame
still burns amongst us
and within,
bringing into being
faith and trust and wholeness
IN THE LORD IS MY TRUE SALVATION…

Loving God, Creator, Redeemer, Sustainer,
look in mercy, we pray
on the brokenness of your creation,
and forgive.

Men: Where we have neglected or abused our bodies
and failed to nourish relationships
amongst ourselves or with your creation
LOVING GOD, FORGIVE

Women: Where we have too easily marginalised those who are sick
or attached labels to them
to avoid the wholeness of their humanity
LOVING GOD, FORGIVE

Men: When we have colluded with under-resourced services
and over-burdened carers,
and patronised people whose bodies or lifestyles
are different from our own
LOVING GOD, FORGIVE

Women: Where we have failed in faith,
trusting only in our own skills
and forgetting you, the great Physician,
and Jesus your Son, the healer of Galilee
LOVING GOD, FORGIVE

AND WHERE WE HAVE NEGLECTED PRAYER
AND FAILED IN OBEDIENCE,

LOVING GOD, FORGIVE

IN THE LORD IS MY TRUE SALVATION…

Song *O the life of the world (Common Ground)*

Reading

From St John 9 (Jesus and the man born blind)
Or from St Luke 8 (Jesus and the haemorrhaging woman)

Reflection

A meditation on the reading, or music or silence

Song *We cannot measure how you heal   (Common Ground)*

Prayer

Let us remember before the God of wholeness
that which we call brokenness
in our world and in our lives

We remember those who bear in their bodies
the brokenness of chronic illness,
of hidden diseases and pains

(Here names may be mentioned)

Voice 1:   I am poured out like water,
              and all my bones are out of joint;
              my heart is like wax;
              it is melted in my breast;
              my mouth is dried up like a potsherd
              and my tongue sticks to my jaws.
              You lay me in the dust of death. *(Psalm 22:14–15)*

Voice 2:   But you, O Lord, be not far away!
              O my help, come quickly to my aid!
              Deliver my soul from the sword,
              my life from the power of the dog! *(Psalm 22:9–20)*

We remember with gratitude and awe
the courage of those who have long-term illnesses
the wholeness of spirit of those with incurable conditions
the wisdom of those who are elderly and infirm
the insights of those who are blind
the sensitivity of those who are deaf
the laughter of those who are dumb
the dignity of those who are dying
the bravery of those who are bereaved

(Here names may be mentioned)

Voice 1:   From you comes my praise
in the great congregation;
my vows I will pay before those who fear him.
(Psalm 22:25)

Voice 2:   The afflicted shall eat and be satisfied;
those who seek him shall praise the Lord.
(Psalm 22:26a)

Let us pray
for all whose courage fails
whose weaknesses overwhelm them
who come close to despair
who begin to hate their lives;
who in the evening cry, 'Would it were morning!'
and in the morning cry, 'Would it were night!'

(Here names may be mentioned)

Voice 1:   My God, my God, why have you forsaken me?
Why are you so far from helping me,
from the words of my groaning?
O my God, I cry by day, but you do not answer;
and by night, but find no rest.
(Psalm 22:1–2)

Voice 2:   Yet you are holy,
enthroned on the praises of Israel.
In you our ancestors trusted;
they trusted and you delivered them. *(Psalm 22:3–4)*

Let us remember all who give themselves
in companionship and compassion
to journey with those who are challenged with different abilities
or who are chronically sick.

(Here names may be mentioned)

Voice 1:   You who fear the Lord, praise him!
All you offspring of Jacob, glorify him;
stand in awe of him, all you offspring of Israel!
(Psalm 22:23)

Voice 2:   For he did not despise or abhor
the affliction of the afflicted;
he did not hide his face from me,
but heard when I cried to him. *(Psalm 22:24)*

God of life,
you give life to all,
and what you give, you never take away.
Take away our eyes of flesh
that look so readily only on outward things.
Give us eyes of faith
to see your life in every human condition.
Strengthen with your Spirit
all who carry heavy burdens,
and all who seek to share their loads.
We pray in the name of Jesus,
remembering his invitation and promise,
'Come to me, all you that are weary
and carrying heavy burdens,
and I will give you rest.

Take my yoke upon you, and learn from me;
for I am gentle and humble in heart,
and you will find rest for your souls.
For my yoke is easy, and my burden is light.' *(Matt. 11:28–30)*

Song *O for a thousand tongues to sing*

Time for the laying-on of hands

Closing prayer
JESUS, WOUNDED HEALER,
BY YOUR BODY, BROKEN ON THE CROSS,
REVEAL YOUR WHOLENESS
IN ALL FOR WHOM WE HAVE PRAYED TONIGHT.
THROUGH YOUR BROKEN BODY, THE CHURCH,
REVEAL YOUR WHOLENESS IN THE WORLD.
AND IN YOUR RISEN BODY,
GLORIFIED FOR EVER,
MAY WE ALL FIND THE WHOLENESS
FOR WHICH WE WERE MADE,
BOTH NOW
AND TO ALL ETERNITY.
WE PRAY IN YOUR NAME.
AMEN

Closing words
To God our Maker
WE COMMEND OUR BODIES AND OUR SOULS
To Christ our Redeemer
WE COMMEND OUR BROTHERS AND SISTERS
To the Spirit, our Accompanier
WE COMMEND OUR WORLD, IN PEACE.
AMEN

A liturgy for those facing serious illness

To begin

Out of our shock and fear
WE CALL TO YOU
Out of our anger and denial
WE CALL TO YOU
Out of our grief and sadness
WE CALL TO YOU
Silence
EVER-PRESENT GOD,
WHERE ARE YOU?

or

Our eyes are heavy with tears
Our minds are racing
Our hearts are like stone
O God,
where is the joy, peace and hope
you promised?
Ever-present God,
WHY HAVE YOU FORSAKEN US?

Silence
(followed by a time to share fears and hopes, stories and worries, if appropriate; a time to be honest with ourselves and with God)

After silence, and/or a time of sharing, everyone receives a candle. The leader lights his/hers from a central candle and invites everyone to light the candle of their neighbour (offering the light as a prayer for them).

All are then invited to say together:

GOD COMES TO US
IN THE WARMTH AND LIGHT OF A FLICKERING FLAME;
IN THE CRY OF A CHILD;
IN THE SMILE IN OUR NEIGHBOUR'S EYES.
CHRIST IS ALONGSIDE US IN OUR SUFFERING.
THE SPIRIT MOVES US TO TEARS
AND DRIES OUR EYES.

Readings, poems, a song (e.g. Kindle a Flame) *as candles are placed in a circle in the centre of the group.*

After a time of silence, the following prayer may be used:

As surely as the tide returns to the shore,
the bird to its nest;
as surely as the sun runs its course,
so surely do I, your God and Lover
return to you.
I will not leave you bereft.
I will weep with you.
I will dry your eyes
on the sleeve of my robe,
release what binds and poisons
your mind and your dreams.
I will come to travel with you.
You are not alone.

Come, Lord Jesus

To die healed

A reflection on contemporary medicine by Tom Gordon, Hospice Chaplain at the Marie Curie Centre, Edinburgh, and adviser on spiritual care to Marie Curie Cancer Care.

Maggie was 58, widowed, and in the end stages of cancer when she was admitted to our hospice. She had soldiered on at home for some time, supported by the caring services from the hospice and community, and greatly sustained by folk from her church, a small, independent church which was deeply precious to her. Now it was time to be cared for in a more specialised environment, because Maggie knew she was going to die soon.

When she arrived with us she was very weak, and struggling with pain and sickness. Our obvious task was to seek to get these symptoms under control so that Maggie could be offered a better quality of life. But it became clear very quickly that the overriding issue for Maggie, deeper even than the problems of tiredness, nausea and pain, and almost certainly contributing to these physical manifestations of her deterioration, was that she was very frightened. The more she realised that death was not far away, the more scared she had become. Coming into the hospice faced her finally with the reality of death, and her fear was extreme.

She asked to see the chaplain on her admission. When I first met her I could see the fear in her eyes. This was more than the usual apprehension about coming to a new place, about hospices and death. (It is increasingly clear, however, that much needs to be done to help people to see that hospices and death are not always synonymous, as they increasingly come in and out of hospices, for respite, symptom control and rehabilitation, and not just at the end stage of life.) For Maggie the fear was all-encompassing.

Her fear came from two places. First of all, she was terrified of a judgemental God. This good Christian lady, who had sought to live by Christian principles all her days, had had the concept of a God of judgement deeply instilled in her over many years. She put it this way: 'What if God finds some sin, hidden away, that I've forgotten about altogether, and haven't ever repented of, then he'll zap me for ever and I'll burn in Hell.' This was no parody. It was real. And this made Maggie terrified of dying.

So, in simple language, with storytelling, the use of images, reference to the Bible, and prayers, in short interactions and long discussions, Maggie and I worked on a reinterpretation of the nature of God, and of a renewed understanding of God's love and forgiveness. It was slow. I thought we were going to run out of time. Sometimes I didn't know what to say. There were bits Maggie found hard to grasp, such was the deep-seated nature of her previous teaching. But slowly she relaxed into the all-embracing love of God, and her fear subsided. This soul in torment found acceptance by her God, and, in so doing, found God's healing power. Gone was the tortured face, the furrowed brow, the restless body. In their place Maggie found peace.

But there was more. Interwoven in our discussions about God and his Love was a searching sharing about Maggie's family life. She had one daughter whom she hadn't seen for some time. Their relationship was chequered to say the least, and there was a lot that Maggie needed to come to terms with about how she felt she had failed her daughter and would not be leaving her with the memories that a young woman should have of her mother. This was unfinished business for Maggie, things that needed to be said, 'sorrys' that needed to be expressed, forgiveness that needed to be heard.

It would have been good if they could have finished the business together, Maggie and her daughter – and perhaps me as well – starting a healing process which for Maggie would have been the reconciliation she needed, and – who knows? – for her daughter creating a platform to cope with grief and the loss of her mother. But, without access to her daughter, it was down to me and Maggie. The culmination of it all was her decision to write a letter to her daughter which was to be left with her things, so that, should her daughter ever turn up, it would be there for her to read. Maggie was too weak to write the letter herself, so I wrote it down for her. We had a few goes at it till it was as Maggie wanted it. It was simple and it was profound. It said, 'Sorry.' It said, 'I love you.' It said, 'Good wishes for the future.' With a shaky hand she signed the letter, 'Lots of love, Mum,' added two kisses, and wrote her daughter's name on the envelope.

What the effect of that letter was on Maggie's daughter after her mother's death I shall never know. But I *do* know with absolute certainty that in the final few days of her life Maggie was at peace with herself, with her daughter, and with her God. She had found a healing of her faith, she had won a victory over fear, she had finished, in the best way she could, her business with her daughter. It is not too much to say that Maggie died healed.

Bobby was a very different person, and yet, in so many ways, he was on the same journey. A miner all his days, he was 72 years old and he was dying of lung cancer. He was admitted to our hospice for control of his pain, but it quickly became clear that this was likely to be a 'continuing care' admission, as Bobby was a very sick man. And we realised that he was not going to be an easy man to work with, such was his aggression and uncooperative nature. Bobby had done little to endear himself to the nursing team during the first 24 hours of his admission. When I met him, he was on his own in one of our sitting-rooms, crumpled in a big easy-chair. He looked grey, and he was puffing on a very thin roll-up cigarette. 'Hello, my name's Tom and I'm the Chaplain here. How're you doing?' I said, offering my hand. He took it – reluctantly – and pronounced, 'You'd be as well buggerin' off, son. There's nae point in talkin' tae me. See, 'am a Marxist and an atheist masel'.' If I'd been quick enough, I'd have said something clever like, 'Well, you'll get a prize for getting *one* right out of two!' But I didn't. I simply said, 'I just wanted to say hello. I'll catch you another time.' And, in all honesty, I hoped I wouldn't have to bother.

The next day there was a message for me. 'Bobby wants to see you – in the sitting room – at 10 o'clock, sharp!' I was intrigued. So I met Bobby for a second time. 'Aye, right son, come in. Sit yersel' down.' (As if it was *his* front room.) 'Now, how long've you got? 'Cos I dinnae want ye tae run away. I want tae tell ye ma life story.'

And he did! – from the age of 13 when he first went down the pit to supplement the meagre income of a large, fatherless family, through years of capitalist exploitation, Union politics, family stresses, picket-lines, drink, fags, religion, friendships, the prospect of death, the lot. It took him an hour and a half. Exhausted, he sank back in his chair. There was a long silence. Then he said: 'Well, son, what do you make o' that? Has ma life been any good?'

At that moment I was at the sharp end of spiritual care, because a craggy old atheist miner was asking a spiritual question – of someone with whom he would never agree in religious terms, but whom for his own reasons he trusted with this sixty-four-thousand-dollar question in the face of death.

'Yes,' I replied, 'your life's been good, right enough. A life's work for better conditions for miners? That'll do for me.'

Bobby died three days later, and with greater peace and considerably less anger than he had showed on admission. More people than me played their part in that. But I know Bobby was on a spiritual journey, sorting things out before he died, 'finishing the business', concluding a search for meaning, purpose, fulfilment, seeking an affirmation of the worth of his life. And Bobby found healing in his search.

Of course Maggie and Bobby were different people, and with very different views of life and death. One worked with religious language and imagery. The other, quite clearly, did not. But both needed to finish their business before death came. In so doing, both Maggie and Bobby died healed.

In hospices we seek to focus on the whole person, not just the part of them which is their cancer. If we are to achieve the best quality of life for each person, the spiritual dimension – the search for meaning, purpose and fulfilment – is as important as all other facets of being.

Of course it is hard to define the spiritual. But Marie Curie Chaplains have affirmed: *'At the heart of being human is a spiritual experience which can be challenged and dislocated in the face of life-threatening illness. The value of spiritual care is the recognition of this dimension in order that people can be supported in their search for meaning, faith and hope, and be enabled to recognise the wholeness of life within dying and death.'*

Everyone has a spiritual dimension and so everyone, in one way or another, experiences challenge and dislocation in the face of death. People like Maggie and Bobby teach me this, as they find themselves physically, mentally and spiritually dislocated to a place where they have not been before – the journey to death. And that's scary! But the value of spiritual care is that *in* this dislocation they can be supported in a search for meaning, and be able to recognise the whole of life before death comes.

In her book *Sharing the Darkness*, Sheila Cassidy writes: *'The spirituality of those who care for the dying must be the spirituality of the companion, of the friend who walks alongside, helping, sharing, and sometimes just sitting, empty-handed, when he would rather run away. It is the spirituality of presence, of being alongside, watchful, available, of being* there.'

It is our task to be that companion, to travel with Maggie and Bobby on their spiritual journey, whatever form it might take. Now that there is considerably greater expertise in relieving the physical symptoms of life-threatening illnesses – the control of pain, the alleviation of nausea and sickness, the easing of breathing problems, and the like – there is a greater need and a greater opportunity to look at other areas of a person's well-being, and to work at the interaction between all the varied facets which make up the whole person. The label is 'holistic' medicine, but it simply means seeing the person as a whole, and recognising that sickness and brokenness in one part can influence and create brokenness in another.

It is not unusual for someone to express their symptoms in physical terms because that is the only language they have to indicate their brokenness, only for medical staff to find that far too small a level of pain-control deals with the pain, or that the patient's pain is not touched at all by a far higher level of pain-control than would normally be necessary. It is what is some-times described as 'total pain'. So we have to ask: 'What is happening here?' and go on to look at whether the pain comes from a deeper anxiety, a fear of dying, a struggle with meaning, an unfinished piece of business, or whatever. In other words, the question is not 'How can I make this patient's pain go away?' but more 'Who is this person? What is happening to them? How does the expression of their symptoms tell us about how they feel? What resources can be made available to heal the brokenness of the mind, the emotions and the spirit as well as of the body?'

Reinforced by expectations of the patient that all ailments can be 'cured' and that with the advance of medical science in recent years even death can be held at bay, *and* by the narrow view of some healthcare profession-als that once the physical is 'sorted' all is well, there can be a tendency in medicine to reduce people solely to that which is dysfunctional in their physical wellbeing. (I once heard a patient described as 'the prostate in the end bed', in one phrase reducing a wonderful old man to one small organ in his body, and a diseased one at that!) But the primary task of contem-porary medicine, focused on by genuine palliative care but, thankfully, not exclusive to it, is to see the 'whole person', to work at the interaction between all facets of being, and to find the healing that can be offered to mind and spirit as well as body.

For Maggie, the body's healing was beyond medical science. Of course her physical symptoms could be alleviated in order that she could have the best quality of life as the dying process took its course. But two things mattered above all else in Maggie's care. The first was that we saw her as a whole person, who needed accompanying on her journey of faith to deal with her fear of the consequences of death, and who needed time to tell her story about where she was with her daughter and so find a way of laying down this issue. And the second was that Maggie herself moved beyond the physical to look at other facets of her life. She chose to use the time and the resources available to find healing for that which could be healed. We did our bit. Maggie did hers. And so she was healed before she died.

For Bobby it wasn't a faith issue. It was working within a Marxist and atheistic framework. But to confine the essence of our being to a religious framework alone, and worse, to insist that people are dragged into a religious framework before they die, is to fail to recognise the spiritual search for people like Bobby, and to say that we have nothing to offer him and others like him.

Bobby's spiritual question was, 'Has my life been any good?' If I had replied, 'Well, no. The only way we can *really* say it's been good is if you "get religion". The only way to heaven is…' and if I hadn't already had a roll-up stubbed out on my thigh, I would have been told to, 'Bugger off with your religion, son!'…and the moment of healing and affirmation would have been lost. The business he needed to finish was to find affirmation of the worth of his life. That is what he got. And there he found healing.

The task of contemporary, holistic medicine is to offer to the Maggies and Bobbys in our care the time and space they need and deserve, the assurance that the whole picture is being looked at and cared for, and the resources to heal that which can be healed.

It has been said that the role of the chaplain in this area of healing is 'to help people articulate their longings'. I would go further and suggest that this should be the role of all who work in health care. If in the stumbling articulation of their longings as death approaches Maggie and Bobby can be helped to acknowledge their brokenness, and if that brokenness can be offered the healing resources it deserves, and which, thankfully, are increasingly available, then to see them die healed will not be an exception but an expectation which can and should be fulfilled.

Service for all souls

As people arrive, each is given a stone to hold for the first part of the service. Have a cross at a focal point, with space in front of, or around it, and nightlights in baskets on each side.

Opening responses
God of all times and places
WE GATHER IN YOUR PRESENCE
God of eternity and each moment
WE TAKE THIS TIME AS YOURS
God of the here and now
WE ARE HERE FOR YOU

Song *Jesu tawa pano   (Common Ground)*
(or a familiar and appropriate hymn)

Reading
Ecclesiastes 3:1–8

Reflection
Look at the stone you are holding. It is unique. Each has a different shape, colour, pattern. Each stone has its own beauty, its memorable smoothness (worn by water, maybe) or rough edges. Some are battered and chipped, some are almost like jewels. Each has a different story, which is in part the story of creation. These stones are inanimate objects – and yet in them the atoms are dancing, as they also dance in us.
Silence
They may remind us of ourselves – and also of the people who have helped to make us who we are. Let us gather the stones together.

While gentle music is played, or a chant is sung (which could be Jesu tawa pano *again), let the people come forward and place their stones in a cairn at the foot of the cross, or in a circle around it.*

If possible, remain in a circle or semi-circle for:

Prayers of thanksgiving *(extempore)*
(During these prayers, nightlights may be lit and placed among the stones as people are remembered by name)

Chant   *Through our lives and by our prayers*
(which may be varied…'through their lives and by our prayers…)
concluding with

Lord's prayer

Letting go
There is also a time to scatter stones, but let us leave these here, even though they may have taken on a meaning for us, and we might want to find them and take them away with us. Let us leave them here, in God's presence.
(The people return to their seats)

Reading
Hebrews 11:13–16

Prayer
God of all creation –
who cannot be contained by our boundaries
or our definitions –
light from beyond the galaxies,
sea without a farther shore;
you are present in every distinct place,
in every moment in history.
You are here and now.
Help us to understand
that those from whom we are separated in life
by distance, by sea and land;
those from whom we are separated
by difference, by prejudice,
by language, by lack of communication;
and that those from whom we are separated in death,
by its long silence, its aching absence –

are each of them in your presence;
that beyond our horizons,
beyond our boundaries,
beyond our understanding,
they are in your embrace.
AMEN

Closing song

Blessing
May God give you wisdom,
may God grant you mercy,
may God give you fullness of life
and guide you, all your life long,
through each day and through the darkness.
AMEN

In our lives they're special
A liturgy for carers

This service may be held as a regular, e.g. annual, event in a church or group of churches, a town or city; and also in a hospital chapel, senior citizens' home, sheltered housing or community centre, especially where carers regularly meet. Special care might be given to how such a service might be publicised, and in what ways carers from all walks of life might be invited and included.

Welcome

Opening responses
We gather here in the name of God
WHO KNOWS EACH OF US BY NAME
We gather in the name of Christ
WHOSE TOUCH BROUGHT HEALING FOR FORGOTTEN PEOPLE
We gather in the name of the Spirit
WHO HAS PROMISED TO STAY WITH US,
TO SUSTAIN US AND RESTORE US

Prayer
Caring God, you have given us hearts to love and hands to care. We come before you as mothers and fathers, brothers and sisters, daughters and sons, friends and relatives who have not turned away from those we love, even in their special need. We are here because we too need your care and love. Be with us, listen to us, forgive us, restore us, in the name of Jesus Christ whose life was care and whose love is everlasting. Amen

Song   *(e.g. Take this moment; Lord of all hopefulness)*

Readings
Let us listen for the Word of God (read by four carers standing in a semi-circle)

Bear one another's burdens, and so fulfil the law of Christ.
(Galatians 6:2)

Are not five sparrows sold for two pennies? Yet not one of them is forgotten in God's sight. But even the hairs of your head are all counted. Do not be afraid; you are of more value than many sparrows.
(Luke 12:6–7)

Are any among you suffering? They should pray. Are any cheerful? They should sing songs of praise. Are any among you sick? They should call for the elders of the church and have them pray over them, anointing them with oil in the name of the Lord.
(James 5:13–15)

Come to me, all you that are weary and are carrying heavy burdens, and I will give you rest. Take my yoke upon you and learn from me; for I am gentle and humble in heart, and you will find rest for your souls. For my yoke is easy and my burden is light.
(Matthew 11:28–30)

Song   *(e.g. A touching place; Through all the changing scenes of life)*

One or two carers briefly tell their story

Address
(This should explore not only the 'goodness' of carers, but also their ambivalence, the conflicts caused by adding caring to other responsibilities, their need to find things of their own to do to maintain a working and personal life.)

Time of quiet

Prayers
Loving God, we remember before you the many kinds of people gathered under the name of carer: those who care for a child whose needs far exceed what is expected, and who will need care for a long time, or for life; those who care for a beloved husband, wife or lover, sister or brother, mother or father, whose health has suddenly, rapidly or slowly worsened; those who care for the victims of accidents, violence or industrial disease. We remember some who care for loved ones with

bodily ailments and some for those whose mental health and abilities make caring essential.

We pray for those who care for more than one person; those who have good support from family, friends and services, and those who have little or none. We remember before you that they all feel under pressure, not able to rest, not understood.

You know all these people; you are the one who hears their voice and witnesses their tears in the dark, lonely nights. Be with them, bless them, and open all our hearts and minds to give them the support they need and deserve, in the name of the one who gave his life for us all. AMEN

We pray for those in national and local government, health and social service administration, who make resources available to support carers. Give them the insight to understand, the compassion not to exploit carers' commitment, the imagination and courage to provide generous support, and to defend the cause of those who care for their loved ones. AMEN

We pray for those who work in the caring professions: doctors, nurses, district nurses and health visitors, social workers, community care staff, sheltered housing wardens, and many others. We give thanks for all the work they do, all the care they show, and we ask that they may grow in grace, wisdom and understanding, especially of people who care for those they are bound to in love. AMEN

We pray for those we care for, and name them silently here… We bring before you by name any who especially need our prayers at this time… Tend your sick ones, Lord Christ, restore to health in body, mind and spirit those for whom recovery is possible, comfort your ailing ones, heal your dying ones to eternal life with you. AMEN

And we pray for carers themselves, in all their frailty and tiredness, in their anxiety, fear and anger, their need for your forgiveness. Open your ears to their hurt and pain, your eyes to their tears, with your loving arms enfold them, grant them peace of mind, restore their bodies, grant them your endurance and hope, and your promise of life to come. AMEN

And we pray as Jesus taught us:
OUR FATHER IN HEAVEN
HALLOWED BE YOUR NAME, YOUR KINGDOM COME,
YOUR WILL BE DONE, ON EARTH AS IN HEAVEN.
GIVE US TODAY OUR DAILY BREAD.
FORGIVE US OUR SINS
AS WE FORGIVE THOSE WHO SIN AGAINST US.
SAVE US FROM THE TIME OF TRIAL, AND DELIVER US FROM EVIL,
FOR THE KINGDOM, THE POWER AND THE GLORY
ARE YOURS, NOW AND FOR EVER. AMEN

Song   *(We cannot measure how You heal)*

Washing of hands
In small circles of 6–8 people, each group has a bowl of warm water, a
towel, and a small jug on a table or chair. Each in turn gently washes and
dries the hands of the next, with a short blessing, using the name, e.g.
'Joyce/Jim, may God blesss your caring hands.' Or, 'May God restore and
freshen your tired hands.' An enabler in each group may help this process
along. If it helps, a chant may be sung, e.g. Ubi caritas.

Final prayers
God, as you have washed our hands
FRESHEN OUR HEARTS AND MINDS TO DO YOUR WILL
God, as you have heard our prayers
BE WITH US AND CARE FOR US IN GOOD TIMES AND BAD
God of all caring, we trust and adore you
GIVE US YOUR CONFIDENCE, YOUR JOY,
AND THE STRENGTH TO SERVE YOU AND ALL WHOM YOU LOVE.
AMEN

Blessing

Final song   *(e.g. Love divine, all loves excelling)*

Carer's song *(suggested tune: Vienna)*

You who know us all by name
on our heads count every hair,
know each sparrow, small and frail,
hear our tired, quiet prayer.

Those we love need special care,
every moment, night or day;
we're the ones who wash and dress,
feed and tend in every way.

In our lives they're special too,
sisters, brothers, husbands, wives,
sons and daughters, parents who
give the meaning to our lives.

Some are dying, some will live,
needing help for many years:
and together we may share
days of peace and nights of tears.

Touch and bless the ones we love,
let them know how much we care,
give them lives they can enjoy,
hope and laughter, dreams to share.

Help us too to feel your care,
rest, restore ourselves, and know
held in your enfolding arms,
we can live, and care, and grow.

The ministry of healing in the life and worship of the Church

Resources for introducing services of prayer for healing

1 Praying for healing
A discussion starter & questionnaire

1. Read out the two quotations below to the group
2. Distribute the questionnaires
3. Allow people five minutes to complete the questionnaire and then
    get them to discuss their answers in pairs
4. Bring the group together and invite questions and comments

When we pray for healing we are asking God to act. There is an expectation that change will occur. When someone is healed physically we sometimes say that our prayers have 'worked'. Such healing may have taken place immediately, or it may have occurred over a period of time and included medical treatment, and the care of professionals, relatives and friends. When it comes to praying for people with deep-seated or longstanding mental health conditions, we are more reluctant to judge the 'working' of our prayers – the 'evidence' is somehow less obvious. It is even more difficult for us if our prayer does not appear to have 'worked' at all. We may attempt to explain the lack of evidence for the efficacy of our prayers. Perhaps we say that God's healing happens in 'his way' and in 'his time' and that we need to trust, rather than define the type of healing that a person requires; or we may feel that such an explanation is a cop-out. Perhaps we decide that our faith isn't strong enough, or that we need to spend more time in prayer. We may decide that God is using our suffering to teach us something new, or we may reason that if we are not too specific in our prayers, and if we don't expect too much, then we won't be disappointed if nothing 'seems' to happen. We may hold back from asking for healing for ourselves, because we feel that others may then expect to see a change in our life, and we will feel that we are somehow letting them and God down if nothing changes.

Whatever conclusions we reach when thinking about prayers for healing, most of us are reluctant to talk about our doubts, fears and sheer bewilderment, or to ask the kind of questions that we think may reveal our lack of knowledge or faith or experience. We somehow feel that we ought to know the answers, and we feel threatened when we know that we don't.

(Ruth Burgess)

Healing is a central obligation of the Church. Christ came neither to save souls nor to save bodies. He came to save people. Thus our whole ministry is one of healing: making crooked places straight in international issues, in class issues, and issues of sex. In Christ Jesus there is neither Jew nor Greek, bond nor free, male nor female.

He is the At-one-ment. And as of the larger, so of the less. Christ makes crooked people straight. As in the body politic, so in the human body. He makes straight, here the crooked mind and there the crooked body, and most often the crooked mind-body.

Just as there is no such thing as 'Christian Truth' over against Truth, so there is no such thing as 'Christian Healing' over against Healing. All healing is of God, and the man who walks again after penicillin is just as much divinely healed as a man who walks again after a service of the laying on of hands. We have no divine repository where 'religious' things happen over against a hospital where so-called merely physical things happen.

We must avoid the danger of 'separateness' – the tendency to concentrate on divine healing as if it can be an isolated recovery, sealed off from social concern. It comes, for instance, somewhere near blasphemy that we should merely pray for 'Margaret, suffering from TB' when we know quite well this illness was contracted in a damp room in the slums of Glasgow. This is not to say that we dare not pray for Margaret till all slums have been cleared. For God is a father, and not just an indifferent guardian of righteousness. He is a God of mercy who saves and heals, while we are yet sinners. But it is to say that it is near blasphemy merely to pray for her individually when there is a known cause which we should be tackling at the same time.

(George MacLeod)

Questionnaire

The purpose of these questions is to help you to explore your thoughts about and your involvement in prayers for healing. There are no right or wrong answers – everyone's answer is equally valid. Please tick the statements that are nearest to your own experience – more than one in a question if you want to. Write in your own answer if you are not in agreement with the statements given; but please keep it short – the whole questionnaire should only take five minutes.

1. How do you feel about praying for others to be healed?

(a) I'm afraid that my prayers won't work ......

(b) I don't know what I'd do if my prayers did work ......

(c) I don't think it does much good, but it can't do any harm ......

(d) It makes more sense to go out and help them ......

(e) It makes God out to be a magician ......

(f) It's something God has asked us to do ......

(g) Other ....

2. How do you feel about asking for prayer for yourself for healing?

(a) I haven't got enough faith ......

(b) I'm not sure I really want to change ......

(c) I'm glad I can ask people to pray for my healing ......

(d) I might let other people (and God) down if I'm not different afterwards ......

(e) I don't want to let anyone else know that there's anything wrong with me ......

(f) I'm not good at asking for help ......

(g) Other ....

3. How do you feel about the ministry of the laying-on of hands?

(a) I find it disturbing and uncomfortable ......

(b) I'm happy to be involved in this ministry ......

(c) I wouldn't touch it with a barge-pole ......

(d) I wish more churches would get involved in it ......

(e) I'd like to take part in it, but I find it a bit scary ......

(f) Other..

4. Do you think there are connections between healing and justice?

(a) I think that healing is a very personal issue ......

(b) I think that healing and justice can't be separated ......

(c) I think that politics and religion should be kept apart ......

(d) I find it much easier to pray for one person than for a community ......

(e) Other..

II Case studies and questions
Making the links between healing and justice

Michael

Michael is 18. He lives with his parents in a maisonette in an inner-city estate. Both his parents work, and his older brother, who is 21, lives locally in a friend's house with his girlfriend. Michael has a history of truancy from school and petty theft, and has spent many months of his life in short-term care, both in social services children's homes and in detention centres. He has sniffed glue since he was eight, initially in the company of his older brother and other boys in his brother's peer group on the estate. His behaviour whilst glue-sniffing is often aggressive. He has never been employed. Michael can be very good company; he is cheerful, intelligent, full of fun, and is generally very caring and loving, and he has a good relationship with his mother.

Michael is at present on the run from the police for yet another petty theft.

Questions

1. What kind of changes in his environment would be good news for Michael, and would contribute to his wholeness and to his hope for the future?
2. How do you think Michael feels about his life? How does his story make you feel?
3. Where do you see positive change and signs of hope in our society that will lead towards healing and justice for everyone?
4. What are you able to do in your own community to bring about healing? How can you challenge the suffering and the injustice that you see happening? Where are you able to share in the healing ministry in your own community?

Michelle

Michelle is 18. She lives with her father and her fifteen-year-old brother. Her father is a long-distance lorry driver and is away from home for long periods of time. Her mother died eight years ago. Michelle is the youngest but one of sixteen children; all the older children now live in neighbouring areas of the city and most of them have children of their own. A number of Michelle's siblings have learning difficulties. Since the age of eight, Michelle has looked after the house and the family, which at the time of her mother's death included her pregnant older sister, her older brother at special school and her younger brother.

Michelle attended school regularly and enjoyed it. She now works locally and is a voluntary member of staff at a local youth club.

Questions
1. For Michelle to survive has been a struggle. What kind of changes in her environment would have made her struggle easier?
2. How do you think Michelle feels about her life? How does her story make you feel?
3. Where do you see positive change and signs of hope in our society that will lead towards healing and justice for everyone?
4. What are you able to do in your own community to bring about healing? How can you challenge the suffering and the injustice that you see happening? Where are you able to share in the healing ministry in your own community?

Jean

Jean is in her sixties and lives in a remote rural area with her husband, a retired small farmer. Their home is a large, old-fashioned farmhouse, which is hard to heat. Their grown family have all moved away to fairly distant parts of the country and have their own successful careers and families of their own. They come for holidays, but she misses them, although she is proud of their success. Jean's husband is not in good health, and she finds caring for him and their home increasingly a strain. Public transport is limited, health services are located some distance away and are not easily accessible, especially in the winter. They have sometimes thought about moving, but they have lived here all their lives, and anyway could not really afford it, and she is reluctant to ask her family for financial help. Her community is an ageing and scattered one, and she often worries about the future.

Questions
1. What kind of changes in her environment would be good news for Jean, and would contribute to her wholeness and to her hope for the future?
2. How do you think Jean feels about her life? How does her story make you feel?

3. Where do you see positive change and signs of hope in our society that will lead towards healing and justice for everyone?

4. What are you able to do in your own community to bring about healing? How can you challenge the suffering and the injustice that you see happening? Where are you able to share in the healing ministry in your own community?

David

David is in his late thirties, married with two young children. He lives in a dormitory town thirty miles from the city where he works. He works for a large computer company which has been 'downsizing' and his job is far from secure. Although he is well paid, he has a large mortgage and he works long hours on top of the drive to work. In addition, he works to constant deadlines and often has to bring work home at weekends. He is constantly tired and irritable, his family time is very limited, and his relationship with his wife, who is at home all day, is becoming difficult as communication becomes less. He knows that his way of life is damaging to his health, but feels caught in a trap of financial obligations and does not know who to talk to. If he talks to colleagues, they might think he cannot cope and his job will be at risk. But he doesn't know if he can tell his wife about the warning signals he has been getting about his health.

Questions
1. What kind of changes in his environment would be good news for David, and would contribute to his wholeness and to his hope for the future?

2. How do you think David feels about his life? How does his story make you feel?

3. Where do you see positive change and signs of hope in our society that will lead towards healing and justice for everyone?

4. What are you able to do in your own community to bring about healing? How can you challenge the suffering and the injustice that you see happening? Where are you able to share in the healing ministry in your own community?

III Issues relating to the laying-on of hands

IIIa Ministry of the laying-on of hands
A general introduction

The Iona Community believes that the ministry of healing is as much part of the Christian life as the ministry of preaching or service, and that the laying-on of hands is a way of sharing physically in this ministry. Important too is the understanding that touch is a basic need of human life; that laying hands on someone in worship or cuddling a child or putting an arm round someone in distress are all ways of expressing our concern for others, and of letting God use our hands to bring comfort and strength and healing.

The New Testament evidence is that both Jesus and the early Christian community prayed for the sick and laid hands on them when they prayed. The commissioning of the disciples in the gospels included instructions to heal and preach. A study of the healing ministry of Jesus can be helpful in introducing the healing ministry to a congregation – as can study of instances where the ministry of laying-on of hands is present within the life of the church today. *(See following suggestions, IIIc & IIId)*

In the West there are many cultural barriers that are threatened by touch, often more so for men than for women. We are also aware that an absence of physical contact, particularly in childhood, can make it difficult for people to give and receive love in their daily lives. Sadly, for many people, touch is no longer the natural experience of life, but has become something that is associated only with situations of distress and times of helplessness, and as such has to be avoided wherever possible. An exception to this is where children or older people are concerned; their nearness to birth and death and their obvious vulnerability often frees us to touch them without fear of hidden repercussions.

Healing services that include the laying-on of hands can be disturbing – even the description 'healing service' can be misconstrued – somehow suggesting that we are summoning God the Magician to our call. For the majority of congregations such a service is not part of their 'normal' worship experience, and because of this is seen as something 'special', in terms of both its leadership and its congregation. This may result in unreal expectations on behalf of those involved and a perception of such services as exclusive. A further difficulty arises within the worship itself when the ministry of the laying-on of hands is sited at the front of the church building, which can tend to alienate and make observers of those who choose to remain in their seats and can only see a huddle of backs.

Within Christian tradition there is a wide variety of ways of practising the 'laying-on of hands' for healing within worship. It can occur within a variety of environments: small group worship in a home, large group worship in a cathedral. It can follow on from a parish eucharist or be part of a mid-week service. The laying-on of hands for healing can be practised by ordained ministers and lay people. The verbal prayers that sometimes accompany the laying-on of hands can be extempore and pertaining to the situation of individuals, or can be liturgical prayer that is shared by the whole congregation. Individuals asking for prayer can come forward silently, or can share the details of their situation with the worship leader. People can come and ask for prayer by proxy for someone they know.

Some people lay a hand on the top of people's heads, others lay a hand on the shoulder, some people rest their hands on the sides of the head of the person they are praying for. Some people lay hands closest to the source of disease or pain. Some lay hands firmly, others practise a lighter touch. Some prefer to sit for prayer, others to stand or kneel.

For those who wish to introduce the ministry of the laying-on of hands for healing into their prayer group or congregation, it may be helpful to experience the practice of a variety of traditions before developing a practice of their own.

The service of prayer for healing on Iona includes both intercessory prayer (including for those not present) and the laying-on of hands. This latter is seen as a corporate act and the whole congregation is invited to share in it. Those who choose to remain seated are invited to join in the words of the prayers.

What actually happens is that those asking for prayer will come and kneel in a circle on cushions laid out in a space in the middle of the church, and others will stand beside or behind them. When the worship leaders pray for an individual they will place their hands on the individual's head, and at the same time those nearest the person being prayed for will put a hand on the person's shoulder or arm. A prayer is then said for the person, worship leaders and congregation saying the words together, often:

Spirit of the living God, present with us now,
enter you body, mind and spirit, and heal you of all that harms you. Amen

Often those not near enough to touch the person being prayed for will put a hand on the shoulder of the person standing nearest to them, as a way of being physically involved in the prayer. When all those kneeling have been prayed for they stand up and let others take their place. They can choose to return to their seats or remain as part of the group sharing the laying-on of hands.

Such a style of corporate prayer, involving the whole congregation, demonstrates that no one person is claiming any special healing power, and that it is God alone who heals. All Christians are members of Christ's body, all a mixture of faith and doubt, all less than whole, and all called to care for each other and share in God's work of loving and healing in the world.

IIIb Touching hands
An introductory exercise

This exercise can lead into a discussion on the importance of physical contact within the healing process, and the laying-on of hands. It needs to be read slowly and clearly.

Find a partner.
Sit opposite each other (or face each other across a pew).
(Check that everyone has a partner)

One of you be A, the other B; decide who is who.

This is a gentle exercise that we will do in silence.
I will be asking you in a minute to touch each other's hands. It's not something we are normally asked to do, and it may feel a bit strange at first...

The person who is A – take one of your partner's hands in your hands, and take their hand palm down on your palms. It might help if both of you close your eyes.

The person who is A, gently feel the back of your partner's hand.
Use the fingers of one of your hands to explore the back of your partner's hand.

Feel along each of their fingers. Feel how each one is different.
See how the sides and the tops of the fingers differ.
Feel the different textures of the skin and nails.
Feel their thumb – you can probably feel the bone there under the skin.

Turn your partner's hand over and feel their palm. Feel the difference between the base of the thumb and the centre of the palm.

Gently feel along the thumb and each finger.

Now take your partner's other hand and gently feel the front and the back of it. *(Allow 30 seconds for this to happen)*

Now hold both your partner's hands together for a moment inside your hands.

The hands that you hold are unique; each finger and each palmprint is different.

Now the person who is B, take one of your partner's hands into your hands, and take their hand palm down on your palms.

Use the fingers of one of your hands to gently feel the back of your partner's hands.

Feel along the thumb and each finger.
Feel the sides and tops of each finger.
Feel the different textures of the knuckles and nails and skin.

Turn your partner's hand over and feel their palm – feel the softness of the palm and the firmness at the base of their thumb. Gently feel along the thumb and each finger.

Take your partner's other hand and gently feel the back and the front of it. *(Allow 30 seconds for this to happen)*

Hold both your partner's hands together for a moment inside your hands.

Their hands are like no one else's. Each person's hands are unique.

Now hold each other's hands as if you were greeting each other
and listen to the words of a Celtic blessing:

> Bless to us O God our sleeping and our rising
> Bless to us O God our hopes and our desires
> Bless to us O God our souls and our bodies
> Bless to us O God the handling of our hands *(Carmina Gaedelica)*

When you are ready, open your eyes and then loose your hands
and take a moment to thank your partner for holding hands with you.

IIIc Suggested passages for Bible study

(It may be helpful if Bible study is imaginative, allowing participants to experience the roles of the people in the stories.)

Old Testament
2 Kings 4:32–37 (Elisha and the widow's son)

Ministry of Jesus
Luke 4:40 (Praying for the sick)
Mark 1:41; Luke 13:13 (Praying for those whom 'religious' people were forbidden to touch)
Mark 7:31–37; Mark 8:22–26; Matthew 20:24–34 (Praying for those who were visually and hearing impaired)
Mark 10:13–16 (Blessing children)
Matthew 17:6ff. (Reassuring those who were afraid)
Mark 5:25–34 (Touching the hem of his garment)
John 13:1–17 (Washing feet)
Mark 6:6b–13 (Sending out of the disciples)

The early Church
Mark 16:18; James 5:13–16; Acts 9:17 (Prayers for healing)
Acts 6:6; 13:13 (Setting people apart for specific tasks)
Acts 19:6 (Receiving the Holy Spirit)

IIId The 'laying-on of hands' in the life of the church
Discussion issues

List and discuss incidences of 'touch' within the life of your church, for example:

- Blessing children
- Confirmation
- Exchanging a sign of peace
- Shaking hands
- Maundy Thursday
- Parent and toddlers group

IIIe The 'laying-on of hands' in daily life
Questions for discussion

When do people use touch to express their concern for others, for example, cuddling a child, making a cup of tea?

What are the cultural barriers that make it difficult to use touch as an expression of concern (gender, religion, age, disability, sexuality, race)?

What reservations do you have about using touch as an expression of concern?

IV Praying for healing
Written requests

The practicalities of inviting written requests for prayers for healing, and of praying for people who are not present within the congregation.

Inviting written requests

When inviting written requests for prayers for healing, there should not be pressure on people to write more about a situation than they choose. A few words are enough – for example, 'for Mary who has cancer', 'for Peter who is depressed'. Some people may choose only to write a person's name: 'Please pray for Michael.' It can also be helpful to let people know that prayers can be requested for communities and situations as well as for individuals – for example, 'Please pray for refugees in…'; 'Please pray for the people living in…'

Pens and paper and a box to receive the requests for prayer or a notice board on which to put them should be made available. A suggestion that people print their requests can make things easier for the person who compiles the prayer list for worship. It should also be indicated when requests will be included in public worship, for example: 'Prayers placed in this box by 4 pm on Saturday will be included in the service of prayers for healing on Sunday evening.' A book in which requests can be written provides a more permanent record, and if left on display can be used as a focus for prayer by individuals. Some people find it helpful to have a physical focus for their prayers – for example, candles to be lit, a piece of wool tied to a prayer net, stones added to a cairn.

Including prayer requests in congregational worship

One of the difficulties that confronts those who lead services of prayer for healing is how to help congregations pray meaningfully for a large number of prayer requests. One option is to copy the individual requests on to slips of paper and distribute them among the congregation. A period of silence or music allows individuals to pray for the person or situation that is named on the paper they hold. These prayer slips may be regathered later and placed centrally, near to a symbol that helps people to continue to focus their prayer, for example, a candle, a Bible, a picture, a cross. If the congregation knows that the prayer slips are duplicated and that another member of the congregation is also praying for the situation on each person's slip, it can lessen the fear that some people have in relation to their inability to pray alone, and reassure them that they are supported in their prayers. Alternatively slips may be given out to small groups praying in different parts of the church.

If the list of requests is long (30+) and the names are to be read out during the intercessory prayers, most people find it helpful if headings are used within the prayers. A congregational response within the prayers, either said or sung, can also aid concentration. (*Examples of headings and responses regularly used on Iona and elsewhere are printed below.*)

Often there are people within the congregation who have not had the opportunity to add names to a prayer list, and it is good to make space within prayers to add names of people or situations, either silently or out loud.

It is usually best to indicate that prayer requests will be included in a service on a particular date, and that if the request is for ongoing prayer, the request will need to be repeated. If this is not indicated, the list for prayer can get too unwieldy to be included in a single service, and people may come to a service expecting to hear a name read out, and be upset if this does not happen.

Selecting headings for prayer requests
When confronted with a long list of names for prayer, it is advisable to break up the list by inserting headings and/or congregational responses. This allows the congregation to focus on the names included in the prayers, whether or not they know the people or situations being prayed for. Unless the congregation is familiar with all the people being prayed for, it is better only to use given/Christian names in the prayers and not include family/surnames.

If names only are given for prayer, they can be divided into groups of eight to ten, and interspersed with congregational responses. If a little is known about the individuals or situations, prayer headings that correspond to their situation can be used *(see below)*. Some headings are non-specific and can be used where nothing or little is known, for example '*Jesus, you knew the joy of God's presence day by day...*'

Examples of prayer request headings and congregational responses

Introductory prayer
Jesus, people came to you when they were in trouble or in pain.
Friends carried them,
strangers told you about them,
some met you walking along the road.
Hear us now as we bring to you those who suffer
and who need to know that you are near.

Headings for prayer requests *(choose those which are appropriate)*
Jesus, you welcomed children and blessed them;
you restored to their parents those who were ill,
so we bring before you…

Jesus, you raised up those who were paralysed,
restored withered limbs
and set those who were ill on their feet,
so we bring before you…

Jesus, you restored those who were sick to health,
so we bring before you…

Jesus, you wept for the city you loved,
so we bring before you…

Jesus, with your words and touch
those who were distressed found peace,
those who were tormented found rest,
so we bring before you…

Jesus, you encouraged those who were lonely, weary and despondent,
so we bring before you…

Jesus, in your words and actions
the oppressed found justice and the angry found release,

so we bring before you…

Jesus, you knew the joy of God's presence day by day,
so we bring before you…

Jesus, in your compassion
you were moved to heal those around you
who were suffering or in pain,
so we bring before you…

Jesus, you recognised the true worth of Zacchaeus,
and loved him into new life,
so we bring before you…

Jesus, you stilled the fears of the disciples
and brought them courage and strength,
so we bring before you…

Jesus, you were moved to tears
when you saw the grief of those who mourned,
so we bring before you…

Jesus, you burst the chains of despair
and opened death's dark jail,
so we bring before you…

In a moment of silence, we pray for those known to us who tonight are
in any kind of need or distress…

Congregational responses
(can be inserted after each group of names)

Spoken
Jesus, to these your people
BRING HEALING, BRING PEACE

You open wide your hand
TO GRANT OUR REQUESTS

God, in your mercy
HEAR OUR PRAYER

Sung
Lord Jesus Christ, lover of all
Trail wide the hem of your garment
Bring healing, bring peace

Lord, draw near, Lord, draw near
Draw near, draw near and stay

Come Holy Spirit, Gracious Heavenly Dove
Come Fire of Love

Watch, watch and pray
Jesus will keep to his word

Kindle a flame to lighten the dark
and take all fear away

Kyrie eleison

Closing prayers
We ask for God's blessing on all who care for others
for those who tend the sick
for those who look after frail relatives or friends
that in caring for others they may meet you and serve you.
We ask for guidance for those who administer the agencies of health
and welfare in this land, that in all they do human worth may be valued
and the service of human need fully and justly resourced.
We ask all our prayers in the name of Jesus who loves us,
AMEN

V The worship environment and leadership

It is important when planning services of prayer for healing to think about the environment in which worship may take place. Some buildings are more flexible than others, but even in buildings of fixed structures, the use of symbols and lighting and the style of leadership can help to create an appropriate focus for people's questions and prayers.

Sensory access

Ask the questions:

- Can everyone in the congregation *hear* what is being said? Consider use of microphones, 'signing', loop system, light on the faces of readers to enable lipreading. When is silence/background music appropriate?

- Can everyone *see* what is happening? Consider stone pillars, lines of pews, use of staging, adequate lighting, use of spotlights. Can everyone see to read service sheets? Consider colour of background paper and large print editions.

- Can everyone *move* within the building? Consider width of aisles, steps, ramps, rails for arthritic knees, enough light to see where you are going. Can people reach the area designated for the laying-on of hands independently?

- How inclusive is your liturgy? Consider gender, disability issues, e.g. 'Please stand (if you are able).'

- Where are you going to *locate* the area for the laying-on of hands and what are the implications? Can people reach it independently? Will they sit, kneel or stand for prayer? Will you use one central visible place or a number of places? If you use an area at the front of the church, what will be visible for people remaining in their seats? (Might it be a row of backs?) Will the congregation be invited to share in the laying-on of hands? Is there room for them in the space you have designated? Have you given clear information to the congregation, in order to enable them to choose how they will participate?

Symbolic action

If you are using symbolic actions within worship, e.g. lighting candles, placing stones, where will this happen? Can everyone see what is happening? Are you using a central space or different spaces around the building? What are the implications of these options, e.g. timing, space to move, crowd control?

The option to refrain from participation is particularly important when introducing into worship something that is new to the congregation. It may help to ask one or two people who are part of the planning group to take the initiative at the appropriate time, and for them to be sitting in different areas of the building.

Leadership

What styles of leadership are appropriate for the worship you are planning? Are one or two people leading/co-ordinating the worship? Would shared leadership be more appropriate? If you are including the laying-on of hands for healing, who will lead this? Can the worship leader and the musician/s see each other.

If a number of people are involved in the leading of worship, rehearsal is essential.

VI Planning liturgies

The drama/story of liturgy follows a similar pattern within all Christian traditions.

A. We approach God
B. We are addressed by God
C. We respond to God's word
D. We are sent out into the world

The table that follows expands on this pattern, indicating liturgical content and suggesting liturgical forms. It also defines the task of the worship leader within this pattern.

The worship resources that follow this section and start on page 135 are split into the following section headings and categorised A, B, C, and D.

- Beginnings (A)
- Approach (A)
- God's Word (B)
- Thanksgiving (C)
- Concern (C)
- Requests (C)
- Offering (C)
- Endings (D)

Sometimes a resource will fit into a number of categories. For example, *God of darkness* (no. 41) could also be used in the 'Approach to God' section (category A), as well as in the 'Request' section (category C). The categories correspond to the Worship Structure table.

When planning worship, it is advisable to begin with Section B, the Word. This can be either a chosen theme or the appropriate lectionary reading. Once the theme is established, the other parts of the pattern can emerge.

Planning and structuring worship is a learned skill that can improve with practice. Studying the worship of your own tradition and seeing how it fits into the pattern described above is a useful exercise in the learning process.

Postscript

Creating liturgy and planning worship is a challenge and a privilege. It can be hard work. For those of us who plan and organise worship, a gentle reminder is sometimes necessary:

> there are times to plan
> and times to leave it to the Holy Spirit
> times to create spaces for God to fill
> and times to be silent
> and to wait and listen.

VII Worship structure

LITURGICAL ACT	LITURGICAL CONTENT	LITURGICAL FORM	TASK OF WORSHIP LEADER
APPROACH TO GOD This is what life is like for us – this is where we're at – this is who You are (we think/know) – this is who we are (we think/know) – we come to you – we bring our hopes and fears – our friends **A**	praise adoration confession repentance forgiveness absolution	song opening responses prayers symbols dance music processions silence	welcoming congregation, helping people say what they want/need to say to God – hope, anger, thanks, despair…enabling people to hear God's acceptance, welcome, forgiveness, absolution, invitation to begin again
GOD'S WORD TO US Jesus…the Word… speaking to us… here and now… **B**	Bible readings related readings (lectionary or chosen theme) recounting past history and present events	readings drama, testimony, dialogue, poetry, silence, story, meditation, dance, preaching/homily teaching/explanation song script/conversation	giving people space to enable them to listen and reflect – getting people thinking, reflecting, engaging…creating the opportunity for people to be addressed by God
OUR RESPONSE TO GOD What hearing and seeing the Word evokes in us, and our response **C**	thanksgiving commitment to God/world obedience change offering prayer for others asking God to meet our own needs hesitation, questioning repentance rejection of God's word reconciliation	sacraments creeds/words of belief prayers songs, dance & music, movement, signs/symbols offering prayers and actions for healing, justice, mercy, reconciliation silence	giving people an opportunity to respond to God's Word to them… to respond as individuals, to share in being church…
PREPARING TO TRAVEL ON… SENDING OUT Going back into the world, aware of and accompanied by the Word. Putting the Word into practice **D**	blessings sending out taking food/resources for the journey…	processions blessings wise words journey prayers closing responses laughter, songs, music leaving songs/dances words and actions to live with…	sending people into God's world, strengthened, renewed, reminded of God's love and care…of God who is in them, around them and ahead of them…

Resources for worship

Beginnings (A)

1. Wise God

Wise God
you are older than the ages,
and you dance in the sunlight
AND YOU LOVE US

Wise God
you shared your bread with strangers
and you welcomed little children
AND YOU UNDERSTAND US

Wise God
you wrestle with the powerful
and you comfort those who need you
AND YOU DISTURB US

Wise God
shining in darkness
felt by those who love you
found by those who seek you
WE ARE HERE TO MEET WITH YOU

2. God our Maker

God our Maker
yours are the hands that traced the rainbow
and hurled the stars into space
COME GOD AND MEET US HERE

Christ our Redeemer
yours are the hands that blessed the children
that healed the sick and broke the Passover bread
COME JESUS AND MEET US HERE

Holy Spirit and Comforter
you hold our hands when we need you
you breathe new hope and strength into our lives
COME HOLY SPIRIT AND MEET US HERE

God our Maker, our Redeemer, our Comforter
you write our names on the palms of your hands
YOU ARE OUR GOD
WE ARE HERE TO WORSHIP YOU

3. God of creation

God of creation
shaper of seas and stars
sender of angels
GOD IS HERE WITH US

God born at Bethlehem
explorer of truths and traditions
bringer of justice
GOD IS HERE WITH US

God among us in joy
healer of pain and of fear
giver of wisdom
GOD IS HERE WITH US

4. Warm, welcoming God

Warm, welcoming God
you shape us and name us
and fill us with wonder
AND YOU HOLD US IN LOVE

Bright, beckoning God
you call us and bless us
and fill us with longing
AND YOU HOLD US IN LOVE

Strong revealing God
you comfort us and question us
and fill us with courage
AND YOU HOLD US IN LOVE

5. God of the shadows

God of the shadows
sharing our pain and our tears and our struggle
draining the cup of what it is to be human
WE WATCH WITH YOU

God of the night
sharing our fears and our prayers and our restlessness
measuring the road between living and dying
WE WATCH WITH YOU

God of the dawn
sharing the questions we never dare ask you
yearning in us for the light of your glory
WE WATCH WITH YOU

Approach (A)

6. Prayer of approach

Lord Jesus
in those days of wonder after Easter,
you called Mary and Peter by their names,
and they recognised you;
and we too draw near to hear our names
spoken in love
and to know you again.

You broke bread with your followers
on the road to Emmaus,
and in the blessing, they recognised you;
and we too come to share your blessing
and your broken life,
and to know you again.

You spoke peace to your disciples,
showed them the marks on your hands,
sent them out to bear witness to your risen life;
and we too come seeking peace,
seeking to bear witness
and to be sent out renewed.

Come among us now,
that we may recognise you
in each other,
and together know your healing and hope.

7. The heart of prayer

Lost in the enveloping
tenderness of God's love
Crying out with longing
for the touch of God
Humbled by the knowledge
of the need for God's redemption
Silent in the face of
the true Word of God
Held in the arms
of God's tender compassion

8. Lord, let us not dwell in the past

Lord, let us not dwell in the past,
nor worry about the future.
We cannot undo what is done,
we cannot foresee what will come.
Let us instead dwell in your peace,
love and be loved,
heal and be healed.
We give the past to you and rest in your forgiveness.
We give the future to you and rest in your love.
We live in your light, open our eyes that we may see.
We live in your love, let your love flow through us,
to the fulfilment of your kingdom.
Amen

9. Inscription

Take from my instep
the skein of damage
that has threaded its way through my life
like a tightening cord.

Take from my body
the wounds of unloving
that puncture and bruise
like a scarring sword.

Take from my mind
the dark engulfing
that has judged my life
like a damning word.

Take from my soul
the unbelieving
that has made you seem
like a lost God.

10. Repentance

Wash me clean, God.
Forget the sprinkling with gentle showers
Tip a bucket of your forgiveness over me
Tumble me in the waves of your mercy
Drench me in the sea of your love

Then hold me
Wrap me round in the shawl of your grace
Warm me and name me
And set my feet
on the road I must go

11. Prayer of penitence: Creator God

Creator God
for our denial of the hurts and injustices of our history
for our wanton manipulation of our geography
for our neglect and abuse of tender and suffering bodies
for our refusal of the responsibilities of mutual relationship
Lord have mercy on us
CHRIST HAVE MERCY ON US

God is good.
On all whose lives are open to change
from guilt to grace
from fear to trust
from resentment to love
God pronounces forgiveness and gives peace.
THANKS BE TO GOD

12.   Prayer of penitence: God with us

God with us
you know our captivity.
We pray for deliverance into your glorious freedom.
When we are inclined to sink into self-pity
or self-righteousness,
confront us with the life of the world
in all its suffering and all its beauty,
and release us into a longing for justice.
Lord have mercy on us
CHRIST HAVE MERCY ON US

When we are driven and relentless
with ourselves and with others,
tied up with pressures of time and money,
release us, through your economy of generosity
into a wider knowledge of value.
Lord have mercy on us
CHRIST HAVE MERCY ON US

When we privilege our own agendas,
hurt others in the effort to impose our will,
or chain ourselves to our fears,
tumble us off the throne of our pride,
and release us into finding our worth in your love.
Lord have mercy on us
CHRIST HAVE MERCY ON US

Lord Jesus Christ,
you know us, you love us, you free us
and then call us to follow you
and we bless you.
Your mercy meets us in our confusion;
may your spirit meet us in our everyday living.

God's Word (B)

13. Woman with bleeding

Shalom: an end to exclusion.
Now, not he the miracle-worker
but she, daughter of the people,
is heroine in her story.

She no longer laments
blood staining her living:
lifeblood flowing from her
like children unborn.

For healing is happening
in their bodies.
The living energy of touch
liberates woman and man
to go out in wholeness:

a brave and rounded humanity
that has the right
to be called divine.

(Mark 5:30)

14.   Canaanite mother

A Canaanite mother came to him
angry and alone; with purpose
but no necessity for meaning,
gut feeling being enough.

The child stayed behind:
a torn-apart self
in her dark world, disturbed
by unresolved relationship;
awaiting the coming of spring
and her own flowering.

There was no escaping her,
this unnamed mother
from a despised people.
She made him listen;
gave him vision
and behind her back
he gave a young life
her own balanced centre
of becoming.

(Mark 7)

15. Jairus' daughter

'Get up, my child!'
This is no time for sleeping.
Lighter than Lazarus,
this raising; his touch
an affirmation of womanhood
amid the misted familiar.

Flute players re-tune
to celebrate the coming
of her bleeding, and the chance
between waxing and waning
of moons, for new life.

Mother and father watch,
unable to do anything
but offer wholesome food
for the journey. The threshold is hers
to cross alone; her knowing
is outside theirs
in the shadow of the unsaid.

16. Wounded healers

Mark

It took a long time for Mark to find a church he could dance in. During hymns, through songs of praise. During sermons sometimes – rocking and turning and spinning in his wheelchair. It took him a long time but finally he found one. 'It disturbs the congregation,' they'd told him. 'Makes people uncomfortable in church.'

'People are afraid I guess,' he told me. 'Afraid of Joy.'

When Mark first started learning he danced in tight circles. God told him how it meant that God's disabled people are afraid, timid. Not loose. Not free. But then slowly, gradually he wheeled and danced and the circles grew bigger. It's not for himself he dances, Mark says. It's for God – to dance in front of God. Expresses his gratitude and thankfulness, and how he's chosen joy finally, and wants others to choose joy too. To dance. 'People just sit in the pews and benches along the back. And when they stand up to sing finally they hardly sway or close their eyes. Like they're crippled and broken. 'Dance and help free the disabled, God told Mark.

We're sitting together making decorations for his wheelchair – tissue-paper streamers, yellow and gold – for the dance tonight. Mark tells me about how he spent six months in hospital with double pneumonia and pressure sores from lying that cut to the bone. Just to move was painful. Getting turned like lying on knives. He cried whole days. Asked God why? Felt like Job. Like Job did. When can I get up again, he cried, like in some psalm and God said: When you learn finally, really learn. He wanted to die, just wanted to die. It was too much pain all the time. At one point with his circulation they were afraid gangrene could set in in his foot and they'd have to amputate. But God said: No, you can't die, I'm not finished with you. You have inner healing to do. Then you can get up. You have work to do but you still won't listen.

'Lying there,' said Mark, 'there's not much to do but think. Think and talk to God. There's no way to get away. You try to, watch the TV and that, but you can't really anyway.'

Lying propped and positioned between locked bedrails, Mark was forced to really work through his feelings from the past: His separation from a woman who was also born with a disability. Their broken relationship, his hurt. His drinking. Above and below all, his broken relationship with God. His anger at God for who God had made him, put him through to suffer.

Then – after six months lying in sorrow, with ulcers and sores eating him – Mark resurrected healed and whole and God said dance. OK, so dance. Stop abusing yourself, stop punishing yourself and others. Stop sitting with words. Dance resurrection. Dance Joy. The good news. Dance for all God's disabled people and for their liberation. Mark doesn't care what people think, he has to dance. It's his purpose, his mission. There's a service tonight, a celebration, and we're blowing up and tying on coloured balloons.

Lately he's been dancing figure eights, Mark says. In the crossing – big, free figures. Flowing, spinning, gliding. 'For a while I was trying to figure out why exactly. And didn't know, so then stopped thinking about it and just danced. Feeling the flowing freedom of it. But then it came to me: If you put a figure eight on its side, you know what it's the sign of?…Infinity. It's infinity. It's dancing infinity.'

I smile and we sit in silence. Finishing up, Mark says to me: 'I wish my mother was alive.' 'Gets lonely?' I say. 'Yeah, sometimes. And the doctors all told my mother, told mom when I was a child, that I'd never walk. That I'd always need a wheelchair…' Mark smiles. 'But they never said I'd never dance. Never said that… Maybe she can see me. Dancing. Dancing now. I like to think of her like that… There, finished, nice huh? Well. I guess that's it. Thanks for the help. So, you dancin' tonight too?'

John 5:1–12

Elizabeth

Few patients in the psychiatric hospital keep track of the days. Either they are unable to – lost in a heavy drug haze – or, since the days are all so similar they don't bother. Elizabeth, who has a fathomless wardrobe, makes a point of dressing up extravagantly. She sometimes changes four times a day! And standing, smiling, in a long, flowing, golden gown, a floppy hat – both too big for the short old woman who looks like a little girl trying on her mother's outfits – long white gloves, bright red lipstick, costume pearls, dangling earrings in the shapes of moons and fishes – she explains proudly, 'I dress this way darling because the days are all the same. And if the dirty old days won't change then, by Jesus, I will.'

Through the long afternoons she dances. In the day room. To a music only she can hear. All around her gather the ghosts of this place – the suicides. The walking dead. I've danced with her sometimes on duty here. She's taught me new steps. Taught me how to open up and hear the music. How to dance no matter what.

Psalm 30:10–12

The rainbow man

Working in a hostel once, I met a man who dressed in bright colours – tie-dyed T-shirts, purple hair, nail polish. Who spoke in colours. It was a depressing, colourless place – dingy, dirty-yellow walls. Clouds of grey smoke hanging. He was labelled mentally ill, schizophrenic. At one time he had taught fine arts at a university, someone said, had worked masterfully in oils and acrylics. Now, he worked in Crayola crayon. Drew like a child, dogs and smiling cats and upside down pink-orange flowers planted in clouds. He got beaten up by the men a lot.

One day he brought in a leaf from a walk he took (he was always taking long walks) and held it up to me and said to look, see the light in the leaf pulsing, dancing still. I was busy and tired and had forgotten how to see, and said, 'Yeah, it's a maple leaf, so what.' I was annoyed and harried, there was someone buzzing at the door again, so many important things to do. 'The light in the leaf,' he said again and danced away in a wind.

And when I sat down and stopped, I realised that what he meant was to look and see that energy, that essence, living in the leaf. He could see it. He was supposed to be disabled but he was able to see the light of God in a leaf and to wonder at it. After weeks of running blind through my life, the rainbow man taught me to open my eyes and my heart again.

John 9:13–17

17. A touching place

She has travelled all her life,
dragging leg irons of disease,
to reach here.

This very spot.

In her aching belly
need has grown to desperation.
It drives her through her terror
and the gawking crowd.

He has travelled all his life
to reach here.

This very spot.

His shoulders ache with the weariness of others,
his brow lacerated by their twisted expectations.

Now her fingers tremble as they stretch
And brush the mud-spattered hem of his robe.

She finds a touching place.

You and I
Have travelled our separate ways to here.

This very spot.

We stumble and trip over
our failure and success.

Driven by our need and compassion
we stretch out tentative fingers
and find in each other

A touching place.

18. I didn't ask to be healed

(Luke 5:17–26)

I didn't ask to be healed;
I didn't even want to be healed;
I'd learnt to live with my limits,
with these legs that don't walk;
I knew who I was
(we have rights now,
an identity to fight for):
I didn't need to be healed.

But my friends thought otherwise,
caught up in their enthusiasm
that you were here, in Capernaum:
'Jesus is here, you must see him.
He must see you, he heals the sick.
The lame are walking –
the lame are walking,
the blind see, you must see him.'

What choice did I have
against the force of their desire?
Arms round their shoulders,
hoisted onto the mat that is my home,
we were up and off early
to beat the crowds
before I could draw breath
to find my voice.

Bouncing me along
they carried me lightly,
faster and further than I dare to go.
I clung on for dear life at times
when we hit the hordes
who had already gathered,
the people pushing and jostling,
calling out your name:

I was afraid of the broken,
the decaying, the dying,
the unseeing, the discarded,
the putrid, the ugly,
the shocking, the despairing,
the unlovely, the unloved,
the crazed.
I'm not one of them.

Who are you that all these people come
thinking you have something to give them?

Who are you that my friends
knew the only way
was to let me down through the roof
– yes, the bloody roof! –
and at that point I'm up
leaning on my elbows, saying,

'Now hold on, this is too far,
just hold on, I don't want to go up there
to go down through there, I don't need
to get close to him, I'll live
without this, I'll live
without this.' But they were already
lifting me higher than I'd ever been before,
lifting me above the heads of the crowd,

Above the windows and the doors,
above the branches of the trees,
above the eaves onto the roof,
and I thought, 'I'm going to die,
I'm going to die,' as the tiles came off.
'They're going to drop me and I'm going to die.'
The red, hot tiles flew all around,
flung far far below,

And the sky opened up around me
(there was a hole in the roof),
and the sky opened up and I went down,
I was let down through the roof
onto the heads of the crowd,
whose hands went up to meet me,
whose hands were everywhere all around me,
lowering me down to the ground

Until I bumped onto the sandy floor.
I looked up and there were my friends
laughing and cheering up on the roof,
and I looked around at a sea of strangers
who had parted and moved back
so that I might be alone amongst them,
with my legs that don't walk.
And then I looked at you.

And you said,
'Your sins are forgiven.'

I heard the hushed murmur of the crowd,
the sharp intake of breath from the Pharisees,
and I thought (and should have said),
'Do you know what trouble you'll cause
by saying that? Do you know people will talk
about what you mean by that
for years and years?
I've done nothing wrong…'

But somehow, strangely, like a rush of God
I knew I wanted what you had to offer.
That for me was the moment,
the moment that changed my life,
not when I saw my legs that don't walk
move, and I heard the startled cry of the people.
Suddenly everyone was praising God
and I was smiling, dazed, amazed,

And yes, I did pick up my mat and go home,
on my legs that don't walk,
but that's not the end of the story:
it's barely begun,
for I knew who I was
and now I've only questions,
questions about who I've become
and where I'm going.

How do I walk alongside my friends now
whose legs don't walk?
How do I tell them what you've given me
without having them look away?
How do I talk of healing
and not of judgement?
How do I know what your disturbing and strange life
in my life might do?

Thanksgiving (C)

19. Loneliness

He died –
you crept in
waiting, watching
knowing that your time would come
when friends had gone and I was left alone.
They went –
you remained
gloating, grinning
knowing that I had no will
to fight you off and ban you from my home.

I bade your sister solitude to hold me in her healing gaze
but you barred the way
I searched my memory for the comfort of far better days
but I heard you say
That time has gone
I am here to stay.

You stayed
but I watched
waiting, praying
hoping that you could not freeze
each morsel of my being with your stare.
Then –
I smiled
for I knew
praising, blessing
loving me through all my pain
in one small corner of my heart – God is there.

And I will let that presence grow
and force you, loneliness, to go.

20. Prayer of thanksgiving

We thank you God for the mystery of your presence here with us.
We thank you for the mystery of ourselves.
We thank you for your sense of compassion.
We thank you for the things of this world.
We thank you for your sense of humour.
We thank you for being you, and for making us – us,
unique as you are unique,
mysterious as you are mysterious,
loving and caring as you are loving and caring.

Teach us Lord to use the gifts you have given us.
Teach us to share them with one another.
Give us grace to use our gifts
to bring healing to the world.

21. A prayer of thanks for the healing of sectarian divisions

Gracious God,
You have gathered us here together from different places,
different traditions
and with different needs.
Of ourselves, we cannot come with undivided hearts;
unfinished business,
unmended brokenness,
the hurts of the past,
the fears of the present,
our torn and weary world itself
all weigh us down.
But you can lighten our hearts,
revive our spirits
and unite us in glad and hopeful praise,
and so we bless you.

For your forgiveness of the harm that we have done

for your healing of our deepest hurts
for your love drawing us together
we bless you.

For your inspiring of our reconciliation
for your power to rebuild our lives and our communities
for your call to journey on together in faith
we bless you.

And in wholehearted praise, we join to worship you
in the name of Christ our Lord.

22. How beautiful is the blossom

How beautiful is the blossom
spilling from the tree,
the hidden primrose
and the bluebell
ringing out the news.
He is risen
he is alive
we shall live
for evermore.
The dark winter is past,
the slow, cold, foggy days are over.
May the warmth of your resurrection
touch our hearts and minds
as the warmth of the sun
blesses our bodies.

23. Creation readings

A. Hildegard of Bingen

The earth is at the same time mother,
she is mother of all that is natural,
mother of all that is human.

She is mother of all,
for contained in her are the seeds of all.

The earth of humankind contains all moistness
all verdancy,
all germinating power.

It is in so many ways fruitful.

All creation comes from it
yet it forms not only the basic raw material for humankind
but also the substance of the incarnation of God's Son.

B. Julian of Norwich

I saw that God was everything that is good
and encouraging.

God is our clothing
that wraps, clasps and encloses us
so as never to leave us.

God showed me in my palm
a little thing round as a ball
about the size of a hazelnut.

I looked at it with the eye of my understanding
and asked myself:
'What is this thing?'
and I was answered: 'It is everything that is created.'

I wondered how it could survive since it seemed so little
it could suddenly disintegrate into nothing.

The answer came: 'It endures and ever will endure,
because God loves it.'

And so everything has being because of God's love.

C. Meister Eckhart

Apprehend God in all things,
for God is in all things.

Every single creature is full of God
and is a book about God.

Every creature is a word of God.

If I spent enough time with the tiniest creature –
even a caterpillar –
I would never have to prepare a sermon.
So full of God
is every creature.

D. Testimony of Chief Seattle *(adapted)*

This we know
The earth does not belong to people
people belong to the earth.

This we know
All things are connected.
Whatever befalls the earth
befalls the children of the earth.

This we know
If we continue to contaminate our own bed
one night we will suffocate in our own waste.

People are strands in the web of life
Whatever we do to the web
we do to others
we do to ourselves

Hold in your mind the memory of the land
as it is when you first see it
and with all your strength, with all your mind,
with all your heart,
preserve it for your children
and love it as God loves you.

E. George MacLeod

Almighty God, Creator:
the morning is yours, rising into fullness.
The summer is yours, dipping into autumn.
Eternity is yours, dipping into time.
The vibrant grasses, the scent of flowers,
the lichen on the rocks, the tang of seaweed,
all are yours.
Gladly we live in this garden of your creating.

F. Seven hard days

This story of Creation can be read simply using two voices. But to be most effective it should have the voices accompanied by movement. That may be anything from one person illustrating the actions of God, to over a dozen people sharing both the actions of the Almighty and the movement of the newly created world.

A: In the beginning, it was very, very dark.
        So God spoke,
        and when he spoke, he said,

God: I can't see a thing!
        Let's have some light on the matter!

A: And so there was light.
        And there was darkness too – just for contrast.

God: A good day's work

A: – said God.
        And that was the end of the first day.

        (Musical interlude, change of lights or pause)

B: On the second day,
God thought he'd do something about the plumbing.
There was water everywhere.
So God had a brainwave.

God: I'll make some dry land

B: – said God.
And so he did.
He said,

God: Shoo!!

B: – to the waters.
And they shooed.
Some became seas,
some became clouds,
some became puddles.

God: Not bad for a beginner!

B: – said God.
And that was the end of the second day.

(Musical interlude, change of lights or pause)

A: On the third day,
God thought he'd make the earth look beautiful.

So he winked at the earth, and the earth winked at him.
Out came shoots;
and out of the shoots came flowers and corn and trees.

God made jaggy nettles and stingy nettles.
He made roses that smell like bath salts
and lupins that have no smell at all.

He made trees with apples on them
which would fall to the ground
and help thinkers to have deep thoughts.

He made trees with smooth barks
so that Joseph could write how he loved Mary.

And when God saw all this loveliness,
he smiled a happy smile.

161

God: Time for bed

A: – said God.
And that was the end of the third day.

(Musical interlude, change of lights or pause)

B: On the fourth day
God thought he'd do something about the lighting.

He needed lights to come on
and help the plants to grow.
But he also needed lights to go off
and help the plants to sleep.

So he made the sun to make white people brown
and brown people browner.
He made the moon to give cats something to sing at.
He made lots of wee fairy lights called stars.
And he switched them off and on,
off and on.

God: This is good fun!

B: – said God.
And that was the end of the fourth day.

(Musical interlude, change of lights or pause)

A: On the fifth day
God decided that he'd have a bit more action.

So he said to the waters,

God: You're going to have a moving experience.

A: And he filled the sea with fishes
                                    wiggly octopuses
                                    and jellyfish –
hoping to find a use for them one day.

And he said to the sky,

God: You're going to have a moving experience.

A: And, in a minute, it was filled with wings –
eagles and swans and sparrows

and the odd elephant
which didn't know what its ears were for.

God: I'm some boy when it comes to getting things to work

A: – said God.

And that was the end of the fifth day.

(Musical interlude, change of lights or pause)

B: On the sixth day,
God looked at creation.

The birds sang for him,
the fish swam for him,
the trees waved at him in the wind.

God: Time we had some life on earth!

B: – said God.
And so it started.

He made creepy-crawlies to curl up inside lettuces.
He made wiggly snakes to lie underneath rocks.
He made chimpanzees which would drink tea on television one day.
He made animals with long necks and paisley patterned pyjamas
so that they could see where the balls went
if they ever played golf at bedtime.

And they all jumped and romped and scrambled over the earth.
It was like a circus without a ringmaster.

God: Wait a minute!

B: – said God.

God: Who's going to take charge of all this?
Who's going to pull out the weeds,
smell the roses
and tell the chimpanzees to behave themselves?

B: Then God had another brainwave:

God: I'll make man!

B: –said God.

God: No I won't!
That would be sexist.
I'll make woman and man.

B: So God made women and men, big and small,
brown and white,
bald and curly,
long-nosed and short-nosed,
with and without freckles.

And then God said,

God: Just for fun,
I'll dare them to get on with each other.

A: God looked around and then sat down.
He was very happy with all he saw.
He was also very tired.

So he went to bed
and that was the end of the sixth day.

B: And he slept and slept,
right through the seventh day.

God: Creation fairly takes it out of you

B: – said God.

24. W(hole)

We're all going somewhere,
(we're all going)
we're all going in, and on, and through, and down
from the womb to the tomb
we're all going somewhere.

We're all going
into the black and the grey,
into the pitch and the dark,
 into the sheen and the shine
 of wet walls

And I can hear the echo of dripping water
I can hear it and I want to touch it
I want to be there where
I can touch the walls of water
and put my fingers in the slivers of silver
in the black and the grey.

I'm going in, going in,
going deeper into the womb, the tomb,
and I know that we're all going somewhere
we're all separately going somewhere together:

Into this mystery,
this awe-inspiring mystery,
where in the dark we can touch beauty
and in our depths find the greatest love.

25. When I risked silence

When I risked silence
I used to imagine you
waiting to pounce on me,
to punish me for all the times
I'd escaped you in noise and bustle –
waiting to sort me out.
Somehow it's not like that any more.
Silence is still scary
but the one who meets me in it
is not threatening any more –
She smiles.

Concern (C)

26. Loving God, be with our family and friends today

Loving God, be with our family and friends today,
hold them in your love.
THROUGH OUR LIVES AND BY OUR PRAYERS
YOUR KINGDOM COME

Be with the poor today, show them you care.

Be with the suffering of our world, give them peace.

Be with the depressed, hold out your hand to them.

Be with the lonely, let them know you are with them.

Be with the homeless, shelter them in your arms.

Be with us and stay with us, we need you, God.
We need you!

27. Our community

What I would like for my estate and children
a community that cares.
a community that shares.
To be able to go on holiday and not worry about being burgled.
To be able to park the car outside without it being damaged, its radio
stolen or it taken away.
To have better facilities for all children, whether from Meadow Well
Estate, Balkwell Estate or Royal Quays.
To have opportunities to gain employment with realistic pay,
instead of benefit that doesn't allow you pleasure and leisure.
To have places to go at low cost or free.
To be able to give a little and then take back when you are able to.
To be able to walk at night without fear of being attacked.
To have organised activities for children and parents of all ages
and all estates.

28. Laughter

You'd have to drag it out of me –
it's a hard thing to do
when you've got problems –
but you've got to laugh
or else you cry
at people's misfortunes –
it would break your heart.

We see others laughing
out shopping
spending money
they look happy –
when you're skint
laughter has to be forced out
like old nails from a wall.

We're all in the same boat here
so we can share laughter –
but let a stranger come
and it can turn to anger
when they're preaching
what they can't understand.

Kids can bring it out
they're the funniest of people
but we've grown up
and know the world
as a cruel place.

29. A prayer to the Holy Spirit

Cursed be the work
that maims children
and destroys parents
and lays bare the land.

And when we forget
the cost of our prosperity
disturb us till we understand
…and change

30. We're all fallen women one way or another

They call it the bungalow
for the gymslip mums
I was really upset
when I heard
my son, getting a fifteen-year-old pregnant,
reminded me of when
I was called a slut
by my family.
I was sixteen
that first time I fell –
chucked out on the streets
to fend for myself
always wandering
from place to place,
roaming, never settled.
Me, I was glad of my fall
glad for a reason
to stand up and fight
for something other than myself.
If you haven't had a good life,
you want a child,
to do it better,
taking that responsibility
makes you grow up.

31. Survivors

1989
Tonight we offered fruit for thanksgiving
Lit candles for intercessions

I offer this fruit in thanksgiving that I am learning to be angry
I light this candle for women who are survivors of abuse.

But God, I couldn't do it.
My prayers would have exposed me.
I hope you understand.

1999
Today we gather together in thanksgiving
Lighting candles as symbols of our prayers.

We acknowledge our righteous anger and our loss.
We acknowledge the process of growth and healing.
I light this candle for all who are survivors of abuse.
I light this candle for the triumph of hope over despair.

(God
it was not you I feared)

I don't want to know

I don't want to know about sacrifice
sin, and death.
Price paid on a cross.
Demands on me.
No.

Jesus suffering with me,
walking beside me.
God knowing, understanding, hearing,
accepting.
Maybe.

A thousand thousand small deaths

A thousand thousand small deaths
blows to my spirit
wounds to my soul
hurts to my body
entanglements of mind
humanity reduced, destroyed.

A thousand thousand tiny resurrections
my spirit uplifted
my soul rested
my body healing
my mind refreshed, enlightened
humanity restored, reaching for freedom?

A new life?
Redeemed?
I don't know.
The specifics of the Christian faith pass me by.
But I think perhaps I'm learning
something of death and resurrection.

A hard irony

A hard irony, either glorious or terrible;
twelve hours after writing
that I cannot accept sacrifice on a cross,
I am distraught because I missed a service
where they sang
'I know that my redeemer liveth'.

Full circle

1989
A worshipping group.
Prayers thought, felt.
Fear
Prayers unspoken
heard by God?

1999
A worshipping group.
Prayers thought, felt.
Fear diminished.
Prayers spoken, shared.
Heard by others.
Heard by God.

I made peace
with my silence.

32. Day in, day out

Day in
Day out
No money
No meaning

Day in
Day out
No security
No strength

Day in
Day out
No work
No warmth

Day in
Day out
God breathes
God listens

Day in
Day out
God loves
God loves me

33. In the days

In the days
when there is
no paid work

In the days
when no one is
willing to hire me

In the days
when the system
grinds me down

Remind me, God
you love me
and you need me

34. Waiting

You go to hospital
you wait all day
doctor comes to see you
you wait again
you go to the ward
waiting
your body seems to shake
your blood goes faster
frightened to
find out what is wrong.

I do not like the smells
the food, the treatment
I hate the needles
doctor comes back and takes my blood
I wait again for the results
my body goes funny again
I just hate hospital.

I like it when I go home
and can say goodbye
to the smell
the treatment
the food
and most of all
the hospital.

35. Healing

For eighteen years I've been locked up.
Like a prison sentence.
From no fault of my own.
An illness which creeps up unexpected
grabbing my mind and soul
I cried out for help
No one there to release or help me
The pain – the tears I shed
Then, one day the prison door opened.
Like a little mouse I peeped out.
Outside were wide-open spaces
My terror had to be faced.
Instead of stepping over all the hurdles
I took the opportunity, gradually
to familiarise myself with my immediate surroundings
There were many changes – myself, for one thing.
Growing old with age
I have woken up from a long sleep
regretting the years I missed.
Yet now, I'm out and about.
Catching up with everything I've missed.
Life is too short and every hour is sacred.
Yet, I'm free.

36. Tweedsmuir

My mother has her mind
but wonders: for how long?
The nurses do their best
but when their homes are gone
old folks lose track of time,
their minds slow down and rest.
Time comes they just let go.
Their mouths become like 'O's.

The others sit around
the television glow
and wander in their heads
on half-forgotten roads
while nurses do their rounds
of pills and teas and checks.
My mother just holds on.
It's what she does: holds on.

She'll stay about three weeks
while she regains her strength
enough to live at home.
She'll make it back at length
but how she longs to speak
about the long ago.
No one is left from then,
the best of life is spent.

These visits pass so quick
and are so long between,
I live so far away.
The time flies past unseen
to steal our parting kiss.
Her brown eyes haven't changed,
they see me to the door.
I've never loved her more.

Requests (C)

37. Special pleading

Once more
to see a snowdrop
to smell the sea
once more
once more
to hold the child
to be a wordsmith
once more
once more
to dance a reel
dive into a pool
once more
once more
once more, O Lord
once more.

38. I hate being ill

I hate being ill
I hate the helplessness
I hate the vulnerability
I hate myself for being like this
I hate you for letting this happen to me.

Soothe me down, God
Help me to hear your voice in the midst of my anger
Help me to trust the caress of your fingers
Help me not to push you away when you come near
Help me to let go into your love

39. Despair is a desperate companion

Despair is a desperate companion
for facing the unknown.
Much rather the funny, dancing
loving partner of my journey,
the spirit of sparkling hope
to lighten my load
and wash away my tears.
Perhaps I'm searching in
the wrong place;
asking the wrong questions.
O God, midwife of my life,
deliver me from anxiety,
dispel my fear,
calm my racing heart,
bring hope to birth again.

40. I struggle with the silence

I struggle with the silence.
Tired though I am,
avoiding silence
is preferable to embracing it,
far less scary.

God at my shoulder,
ready to rock me,
to calm me,
to hold me close,
let me
let you
meet my need.

41. God of the darkness

God of the darkness
we are afraid
There are dangers and memories
that hurt us and harm us
We are scared of the dark.

God of the night
we are restless
There are snares and distractions
that lure us and trap us
We are wary of the night.

God of the shadows
we are uncertain
There are questions and risks
in believing your promise
We are uneasy in the shadows.

Come, God of the night
come in the sun that is rising
shine in the darkness and scatter the shadows
Come warm us with love and with light.

42. Come with us God

Come with us God,
come into the desert
the painful and lonely places
of our memories
of our lives.
Come with your angels
and bring us peace

43. The visit

Take me by the hand
Hold fast to me
End my apprehension and stay
Very close while
I walk silently through the ward and
Sit beside someone who means a lot
I know the time is near and I am afraid
Take me by the hand

Offering (C)

44. Dedication to the Holy Spirit

Creator Spirit,
You produce good fruits;
not blueprints for perfection, but love and joy,
not lust for possession but peace and patience,
not striving for superiority but goodness and faithfulness,
not hard self-righteousness but kindness and humility,
not power play but self-discipline.

We offer you the fruits of our lives,
our insights for reflection,
our intentions for action,
our money, time and talents.
In you and through you,
let them be healing, nourishing, serving
in the life of the world.

Touch us with your loving and joyful spirit,
deliver us to be your new creation
and sharers in your creativity
so that we may be people who choose life not death.

45. The work of our hands

May the work of our hands show to all
our love of you and our love for others.
May your hand guide the skilful work
of our doctors and surgeons.
May the good things of the earth, given by you,
be used to bring health and wholeness in our medicines and remedies.
May we recognise the care of your angels
in our medical staff and nurses.
May the reality of your kingdom on earth
be found by all seeking peace and healing.

Loving God, fulfil your purposes in us all,
that in joy or sorrow, in hurt or healing,
we may come before you as your children
in the sure knowledge of your love for us.
Amen

46. Prayer for three voices

Voice 1:
God of justice, keep us silent
when the only words we have to utter
are ones of judgement, exclusion or prejudice.
Teach us to face the wounds in our own hearts
(Silence)
GOD OF JUSTICE, GIVE US POWER OF SPEECH
TO RESIST INJUSTICE, OPPRESSION AND HATE,
NOT ONLY ON OUR OWN BEHALF
BUT FOR OTHERS WHO ARE NOT HEARD.
MAKE US PEACEMAKERS AND RESTORERS OF THE STREETS.

Voice 2:
God of power, keep us silent
so that we may listen respectfully
to another person's pain
without trying to fade or fix it,
for you are present within each one of us
(Silence)
GOD OF POWER, GIVE US COURAGE
TO SHARE OUR GIFTS OF SPEECH
TO COMFORT, UPHOLD AND STRENGTHEN.
LET US BE A GLIMPSE OF YOUR LOVE TO THOSE IN NEED.

Voice 3:
God of love, in the silence of our hearts
give us words of welcome, acceptance and renewal
so that when we speak
our words come from you

(Silence)
GOD OF LOVE, GIVE US VOICES OF PRAISE
TO CELEBRATE EACH OTHER
AND THE GLORIES OF CREATION
BELIEVING THAT WE ALL LIVE WITHIN YOUR BLESSING.

47. Prayer of joyful access

Jesus, brother, you sat down at table
with women who sold their bodies,
men who sold their souls,
and those whose lives were traded by strangers.
You ate with them,
and when you broke the bread
wine and laughter flowed.
AS WE FEAST WITH YOU NOW
MAY YOUR BREAD STRENGTHEN US
YOUR WINE WARM US
AND YOUR LOVE CHEER US FOR THE DAYS TO COME.
AMEN

48. Separation

I have a cherry tree in my garden.

The roots and the base of the trunk are from a tree that provides strength – a source to build roots of support, to feed and nourish the tree for growth.

Two other different young trees could not grow well on their own. They were not strong enough to develop their own firm roots or to help their own fruit and seeds develop well. So they were joined together. Both grafted onto the one strong root and trunk – given by God to join them together and to enable them to grow and bear fruit.

But over the years, one has grown tall and straight to the sun, the other has grown stretching wide and low across the garden. Both have their own growth and space, but, against expectation, they have not intertwined their centre or their branches. They have looked and grown in different ways and now are hindering one another.

It is time to be set apart.

This is not easy for either, and it will mean they have to begin again; to be cut down, to be grafted again but this time separately, trusting the gardener.

It will mean beginning again, letting go of the past to begin the future. To begin again, but with a greater understanding of what can be hoped and worked for.

Lord, each of us has grown from a seed in your garden.

Many of us have been grafted together in relationships and marriage by you, and for many, being grafted together has enabled us to grow, support and intertwine with one another in love.

But we know that, for some of us, our growth together has not interwoven our branches, but conflicted and tangled our growth.

Lord, we know that only you can join us together,
and that our life and growth and experience together can never be
undone or broken.

Pulled away from our root in you would mean that we both would die.

So it is only of you Lord that we can ask
that the growth we had together may not be lost,
but that now we may separate to be grafted anew,
rooted in you,
with new possibilities for growth.

Lord, we offer ourselves to you, putting our trust in you.
Amen

Endings (D)

49. Teach us to number our days that we may apply our hearts to wisdom *(Ps. 90)*

Bless to me, O God,
this day, fresh made.
Bless me in the lowing of cattle
and the rumble of traffic.
Bless me at desk or helm
and in the confines of my room.
Bless me in the comfort and constriction of my bed
and in the prayer I offer.

Bless the unknown ones
for whom I pray:
the victims of terrorism
and the perpetrators of it;
those swept to extinction
by fire or flood – thousands
and yet each one known
and precious to You.

Bless me in my journey, Christ
through this day
and through this life
till this day ends
and a new day dawns.

50. With the love of God

With the love of God
MAY WE BE WARMED AND WELCOMED
With the justice of Jesus
MAY WE BE CHALLENGED AND MADE WHOLE
With the breath of the Spirit
MAY WE BE FILLED WITH COURAGE AND LIFE. AMEN

51. May God the Maker bless us

May God the Maker bless us
MAY WE GROW WISE AND STRONG AND HOLY
May God the storyteller bless us
MAY WE KNOW LAUGHTER AND GRACE AND HEALING
May God the life-breather bless us
MAY WE BE FILLED WITH CURIOSITY AND COURAGE AND LOVE. AMEN

52. Beckon us God

Beckon us God
with your smile of welcome
with your strong, sure calling
BECKON US IN THE MORNING

Challenge us God
with your love and justice
with your truth and travelling
CHALLENGE US IN THE NOONTIDE

Keep us God
with your saints and angels
with your friends and children
KEEP US IN THE EVENING

Cradle us God
with your songs and stories
with your hope and healing
CRADLE US TILL DAWNING. AMEN

53. Come bless us God

Come bless us God
bless us with tears and laughter
BLESS US WITH LOVE

Come bless us Jesus
bless us with hope and healing
BLESS US WITH LOVE

Come bless us Holy Spirit
bless us with creativity and wisdom
BLESS US WITH LOVE. AMEN

54. Loving and compassionate God

Loving and compassionate God
you lead your children homewards;
secure in our relationship with you
may we be reconciled with one another
and bear witness to your glory in the world.

55. In the business of our days

In the business of our days
challenge us with your integrity and grace
and enfold us always in your strong healing love.

56.   May the God who dances

May the God
who dances
in the storms
and the sunlight
keep you
and cherish you
in mercy
and love.

57.   May God bless you

May God bless you.
May you be holy and strong and creative
May you know the joy of Jesus
May you dance in the wildness of the Spirit's breath.
May God's glory continue to grow in you
gently, powerfully, tenderly.
May you be cradled in warmth and healing
May you be held in God's wisdom and love.

58.   May the blessing of God surround us

May the blessing of God surround us
May angels and friends share our journey
May we be wise and strong and creative
May we celebrate life and hope.
May God's image grow within us
May laughter and courage heal us
May the gospel of life sustain us
All the days of our journey home

59. The blessing of God be ours

The blessing of God be ours
Warmth and courage
and strength and healing
all the nights and days
of our journey home. AMEN

60. O Pilgrim God

O Pilgrim God
Come with us on our journey
Come with your saints and prophets and angels
Come with your bread and wine and stories
Come be our light, our hope, our healing
Come lead us safely home. AMEN

Index of resource titles and authors

Index of authors and contribution numbers

Index of songs and chants

HSNW   *Heaven Shall Not Wait* (Wild Goose Songs, vol. 1)
EOA   *Enemy of Apathy* (Wild Goose Songs, vol. 2)
MAG   *Many and Great: Songs of the World Church* (vol. 1)
All published by Wild Goose Publications, Glasgow

CG   *Common Ground: A Song Book for All the Churches* (Saint Andrew Press, 1998, Edinburgh)

Amazing grace; God's got the whole world; In the Lord is my true salvation (Taizé); Through all the changing scenes of life
The above songs are not published by Wild Goose Publications, but are widely anthologised.

I bind unto myself today; Lord of all hopefulness; Love divine, all loves excelling; O for a thousand tongues to sing
from *The Church Hymnary*, 3rd edition, 1973, OUP

This is my song © Kathy Galloway 1999

You who know us all by name © Anna Briggs 1999